From Brokenness To Beauty Written By The Pen of Grace

Joshua Rhoades

Published by Joshua Paul Rhoades, 2024.

FROM BROKENNESS TO BEAUTY WRITTEN BY THE PEN OF GRACE

First edition. September 30, 2024.

Copyright © 2024 Joshua Rhoades.

ISBN: 979-8227512499

Written by Joshua Rhoades.

Also by Joshua Rhoades

Courage Under Fire: David's Stand On The Battlefield
Jonah's Journey: Voices Of Redemption And Lessons In Obedience
The Furnace Of Faith: 12 Principles From The Heat Of Faith
Whispers of Hope: Inspiring Stories of Men's Prayers In Scripture
Frontier Legends: The Oregon Dream
Elijah: A Beacon Of Boldness
HOOK, LINE & SAVIOUR - Faith Reflections from Fishing
Driven By Faith: Motor Racing Inspired Christian Life
30 Day Devotional - Bold and Strong- Coffee Devotions for a Courageous
Christian Walk
Authentic Christianity: The Heart of Old Time Religion
Consider The Ant - God's Tiny Preachers
Flee Fornication: The Plea For Purity
Renewed Hope- How to Find Encouragement in God
Sounding The Call - The Voice of Conviction
The Altar - Where Heaven Meets Earth
The Bible's Battlefields- Timeless Lessons from Ancient Wars
The Sacred Art of Silence - How Silence Speaks in Scripture
Under Fire- The Sanctity of the Traditional Biblical Home
Who Is on the Lord's Side? A Call to Righteousness
What Is Truth? - From Skepticism to Submission
First and Goal- Faith and Football Fundamentals
From Dugout to Devotion- Spiritual Lessons from Baseball
Par for the Course- Faith and Fairways
The Believer's Pace- Tools for Running Life's Marathon
The Immutable Fortress- Security in God's Unchanging Nature
Biblical Bravery
Deer Stands and Devotions: A Hunter's Walk with God

Jesus Knows- Our Hearts, Our Responsibility

Restoration - Setting The Bone

Spiritual 911- God's Word for Life's Emergency's

The Freedom of Forgiveness

The Jezebel Effect - Ancient Manipulations Modern Lessons

The Shout That Stopped The Saviour

The Time Machine Chronicles: Old Testament Characters

Anchored In Truth Exploring The Depths of Psalm 119

Biblical Counsel on Anger

Proverbs' Portraits The Men God Mentions

Stumbling in the Dark - The Dangers of Alcohol

Guarding the Wicket Protecting Your Faith and Game

The Champion's Faith - Wrestling and Achieving Spiritual Victory

Scriptural Commands for Modern Times Living God's Word Today Volume 1

Scriptural Commands for Modern Times Living God's Word Today Volume 2

Scriptural Commands for Modern Times Living God's Word TodayVolume3

The Greatest Gift

A Christmas Journey of Faith

Daughter Of The King: Embracing Your Identity In Christ

Determination and Dedication Building Strong Faith As A Young Man

Walking Through Walls God's Power to Part the Storms of Life

David's Song Of Deliverance Praising God Through Every Storm

From Weakness to Warrior: Gideon's Transformation

Why Did Jesus Weep?

Living For God The Call To Be A Living Sacrifice

My Mind Is In A Fog What Do I Do?

Turning The Page Written By Grace

The Calling and Greatness of John the Baptist

For Such a Time Esther's Courageous Stand

From Brokenness To Beauty Written By The Pen of Grace

Dedication

To you, the reader of "From Brokenness to Beauty: Written by the Pen of Grace", this journey is for you. It is for every heart that has felt the weight of brokenness, for every soul that has questioned whether they could ever be whole again. This book is dedicated to you who have faced seasons of pain, regret, or loss so deep that it felt like the story of your life had been irreparably shattered. You are not alone. In those moments of brokenness, when all seems lost, God's grace is still writing your story. His hand, steady and faithful, never lets go of the pen, even when you cannot see what He is doing.

I want to challenge you as you read these pages to embrace the truth that your brokenness is not the end of your story—it is the beginning of something far more beautiful. God doesn't erase the hard parts of our lives, but He redeems them in ways we cannot comprehend. Every wound you carry, every regret that lingers, and every mistake you've made is an opportunity for God to show His transformative love. Let these pages remind you that He is the ultimate author, turning even the most painful chapters into testimonies of His unrelenting grace and mercy.

It's not easy to believe in beauty when all you see is brokenness. But I encourage you to trust that God's grace is sufficient. The journey of transformation may not be quick, and the process may not always make sense, but His grace never fails. With every tear you've shed, every struggle you've faced, and every failure you've endured, He is there, weaving a story that glorifies His love and healing power.

Allow this book to challenge you to see beyond the surface of your pain and look deeper into what God is doing in your life. He is not finished with you yet. The pen of grace is still writing, and the next chapter is one of redemption, hope, and beauty. Let this book be a reminder that no matter where you've been or what you've done, God is more interested in where He is taking you. You are not defined by your brokenness—you are defined by His love.

So, dear reader, as you walk through these pages, let your heart open to the possibility of transformation. Let go of the shame, the fear, and the doubts, and step into the truth that God's grace is working all things together for good. This book is for you, written in the hope that you will see yourself through the eyes of grace and discover that beauty is being made from the ashes of your past. You are a masterpiece in progress, and God's love will carry you through to a future more glorious than you can imagine. This is your story, written by the pen of grace. Embrace it.

Introduction

"From Brokenness to Beauty: Written by the Pen of Grace" is a journey into the heart of God's redemptive love, a love that takes the shattered pieces of our lives and writes a story far greater than we could ever imagine. We all have moments of brokenness—times when we've felt lost, defeated, and unsure of how to move forward. Whether through our own mistakes, life's unexpected trials, or the pain inflicted by others, we carry wounds that seem too deep to heal, regrets that feel too heavy to lift. But this book is a reminder that no matter how broken we may feel, God's grace has the power to transform our pain into beauty, to rewrite the narrative of our lives with His love.

Grace is not just a word; it is the very essence of who God is. It is His unmerited favor, His relentless mercy, and His unshakable commitment to us, even in our darkest moments. Through every failure, every tear, every mistake, God's grace is at work, taking what seems beyond repair and turning it into something beautiful. This book will challenge you to see your brokenness through the eyes of grace, to trust that God is not done with you, and to believe that your story—no matter how messy or incomplete—can be rewritten by His hand.

In these pages, you will encounter the truth that God doesn't erase the hard parts of our lives; He redeems them. He doesn't discard the broken chapters, but instead, He uses them to showcase the beauty of His love and the depth of His healing. "From Brokenness to Beauty: Written by the Pen of Grace" invites you to embrace the process of transformation, to trust in the pen of God's grace, and to discover how God can take even the most painful parts of your story and turn them into a testimony of His unending faithfulness. Let this be the start of your journey from brokenness to beauty, written by the loving hand of God's grace.

Chapter 1

"Grace holds the pen as God continues to write, turning our darkest nights into His shining light."

Grace holds the pen, and with each stroke, God continues to write a story far beyond our understanding, taking the darkest nights of our lives and turning them into His shining light. Imagine for a moment that life is a vast, unfinished book, and we are characters within it, living through chapters that we often don't understand. We stumble through the pain, uncertainty, and fear, wondering how the plot of our lives will unfold, but what we must always remember is that God is the Author, and grace is His instrument. It is grace that carries the story forward, grace that smooths over the rough edges of our mistakes, and grace that transforms even the most hopeless of circumstances into something beautiful. When we face those nights where everything feels lost, when the darkness seems so thick that we can't see a way out, grace is already at work, quietly turning the page, already writing the next line where light will break through. There is no darkness too deep, no pain too great that God's grace cannot reach. In the midst of our darkest moments, God is not distant or uninvolved—He is right there, pen in hand, writing His light into our story, weaving redemption into every tear, every heartbreak, and every failure. Sometimes we may feel as though our lives are filled with chaos, as though the narrative has gone off course, but that is when grace is most powerful, turning what seems like a tragedy into a testimony of His goodness. Grace does not ignore the pain or brush aside the struggles; rather, it takes the very things that threaten to undo us and uses them to shape us into something more radiant, something more reflective of His light. Grace is the hand of God that reaches into our mess, our confusion, our sin, and our suffering, and pulls out beauty from the ashes. It's the soft whisper in the night that tells us we are not alone, that the story is not over, and that even in the darkest of times, God is working behind the scenes, writing light into our lives in ways we cannot yet see. As the Author, God knows every detail, every thought, and every fear that we carry, and He uses His grace to redeem it all, to turn the very moments of despair into the moments where His light shines the brightest. Grace is patient. It waits for us to understand, to see, and to trust that the Author's hand is steady, that He knows where the story is going even when we do not. Grace is not a quick fix or a bandaid over our pain, but rather, it is the relentless love of God, the determination to turn even the most painful of circumstances into something that will bring Him glory and bring us peace. There is no moment too dark that grace cannot reach; no chapter too painful that grace cannot rewrite. When we face our darkest nights, it's easy to feel abandoned, forgotten, or lost in the shadows, but the truth is that God is never closer than in those moments. His grace is not just a passive force, but an active and powerful pen, moving through the pages of our lives, writing light into the places where we thought light could never reach. It's in the darkest nights that we often learn the most about grace, for it's when we are most in need that we see just how deep God's love for us truly goes. Grace doesn't just meet us where we are; it transforms us. It turns fear into courage, doubt into faith, and sorrow into joy. It takes the broken pieces of our lives and makes them whole again, not by erasing the past, but by redeeming it, by turning even our worst moments into a testimony of His love and power. And as God continues to write, He does so with a vision of the end that we cannot yet see. What seems like a never-ending night to us is just a chapter in a much larger story—a story where His light will eventually shine through, where every tear will be wiped away, and where every broken heart will be healed. The beauty of grace is that it doesn't wait for us to have it all together. It meets us in our weakness, in our failure, in our darkest nights, and it turns those very things into the places where God's light shines the brightest. When we feel like we've reached the end of our rope, when we feel like we've made too many mistakes or fallen too far, grace reminds us that the story isn't over. God is still writing. He's still at work, even when we can't see it, turning our darkest nights into His shining light. This is the incredible hope that grace gives us—that no matter how dark the night may seem, morning is coming. Light is coming. Redemption is coming. The very things that the enemy meant for our destruction, God will use for our good. And He does it all through grace. Grace is the pen that God uses to write beauty into our brokenness, to write hope into our despair, and to write love into every corner of our hearts. It's the assurance that, no matter what happens, no matter how many times we fall or fail, God's grace will always be there to pick us up, to continue writing our story, and to bring us into the light of His love. Every night has an end, every dark moment has a dawn, and every broken heart can be healed by the grace of God. The world around us may be filled with uncertainty, pain, and darkness, but we can rest in the knowledge that God is still in control, that He is still writing, and that His grace will always turn our darkest nights into His shining light. The story of our lives is not defined by the darkness we face, but by the grace that carries us through it. Grace is what turns tragedy into triumph, what takes the darkest moments and uses them to bring about the brightest light. When we feel lost, broken, or abandoned, we can trust that God's grace is already at work, writing a new chapter, one that will bring hope, joy, and light into the darkest corners of our lives. And as He continues to write, we can be confident that the story He is writing is one of redemption, one of grace, and one where His light will always overcome the darkness. In the end, it is grace that holds the pen, and as long as grace is writing our story, we can trust that no matter how dark the night may seem, light will always come. The darkness cannot last, because God's grace is too powerful, too relentless, too full of love to leave us in the shadows. So, as we walk through the darkest nights, let us remember that grace is at work, that God is still writing, and that His light will always break through. Grace turns our darkest nights into His shining light, and for that, we can trust Him with every part of our story.

Chapter 2

"Even when we stumble, God's grace pens the next chapter with love and redemption."

Even when we stumble, God's grace pens the next chapter with love and redemption. Imagine for a moment that our lives are like books, with each chapter filled with the stories of our triumphs and our failures. There are moments of joy and moments of sorrow, times when we feel like we are walking in the light and other times when we stumble and fall, feeling lost in the darkness. But through it all, one thing remains constant: God's grace. His grace is like a masterful author who never gives up on the story, who keeps writing, even when we think the story is over, even when we have made a mess of things and believe that our mistakes have ruined everything. No matter how far we've fallen or how badly we've stumbled, God's grace is always there, ready to write the next chapter of our lives, and it's a chapter filled with love and redemption.

When we stumble, it's easy to feel like we've failed, like we're not good enough, like our mistakes define us. We may feel unworthy of love, unworthy of God's forgiveness, and unsure of how to move forward. But here's the incredible truth: God's grace is not dependent on our perfection. He doesn't require us to be flawless or to have it all together. He knows that we will stumble. He knows that we will make mistakes, and yet, His love for us never wavers. His grace is there, not to condemn us, but to lift us up, to brush the dust off our feet, and to help us take the next step forward. He doesn't discard us because of our mistakes. Instead, He lovingly writes a new chapter, one where our failures are not the end of the story but the beginning of something beautiful, something redeemed.

God's grace is so much greater than we can ever fully comprehend. It is not limited by our human understanding of love and forgiveness. While we may be quick to hold grudges or to struggle with forgiving ourselves and others, God's grace operates on an entirely different level. It is unconditional, unrelenting, and unfathomably deep. When we stumble, God doesn't look at us with disappointment or frustration. Instead, He looks at us with love—love that is so vast and overwhelming that it pours out into every aspect of our lives, rewriting even the darkest chapters with the light of His redemption.

There are moments in life when we fall short, and the weight of our mistakes can feel overwhelming. We may feel as though we've disappointed God, that we've strayed too far from His path, that we've made too many mistakes to ever be forgiven. But God's grace reminds us that we are never too far gone for Him to reach us. No mistake is too big, no stumble too great, for His grace to cover. When we fall, God's grace is already there, ready to catch us, ready to turn our mistakes into opportunities for growth and redemption. His grace is like a loving parent who, when a child falls while learning to walk, doesn't get angry or frustrated but instead lovingly picks the child up, encourages them, and helps them try again.

God's grace doesn't just leave us where we are. It meets us in our brokenness, in our stumbling, and then gently leads us forward. It doesn't erase the past, but it redeems it, taking even our worst moments and using them for good. Every time we stumble, God's grace steps in to write a new chapter, one that is filled with love, forgiveness, and the promise of redemption. It is a chapter where our mistakes are not the end, but the beginning of a beautiful transformation. It is a chapter where God shows us that His love is greater than our failures, that His redemption is more powerful than our sin.

We are often our own worst critics. When we stumble, we tend to beat ourselves up, replaying our mistakes over and over in our minds, believing that we are defined by our failures. But God's grace tells us a different story. His grace tells us that we are defined not by our mistakes but by His love. It tells us that no matter how many times we fall, He is always there to lift us back up, to guide us forward, and to remind us that His plans for us are not destroyed by our failures. God is the author of our lives, and His grace is the pen that writes the story of love and redemption, no matter how many times we stumble along the way.

In every chapter of our lives, God's grace is present. It is present when we are walking confidently in our faith, and it is present when we stumble and fall. His grace doesn't abandon us in our weakness; rather, it shines brightest in those moments. When we stumble, we are reminded that we cannot do this life on our own. We are reminded of our need for God, of our need for His grace to guide us, to strengthen us, and to carry us forward. And in those moments, God's grace steps in, not with judgment, but with love. He lovingly writes the next chapter of our lives, a chapter that is marked not by our failures but by His redemption.

God's grace is not only about forgiveness—it is about transformation. It takes our stumbling and turns it into an opportunity for growth. It takes our mistakes and uses them to refine us, to make us more like Christ. God's grace doesn't just cover our sins; it transforms us from the inside out, making us new. Every time we stumble, every time we fall short, God's grace is there, writing a new chapter, one that draws us closer to Him, one that teaches us more about His love and His mercy.

Even when we stumble, God's grace pens the next chapter with love and redemption. It is a grace that never gives up on us, never walks away, and never says, "This is the end." Instead, it says, "Let's begin again." It says, "I will take your mistakes, your failures, and your brokenness, and I will turn them into something beautiful." God's grace is the pen that keeps writing, even when we feel like giving up, even when we think we've messed up too badly to continue. His grace writes a story that is filled with second chances, with new beginnings, and with the overwhelming love of a God who never stops pursuing us.

God's grace is relentless in its pursuit of us. It doesn't stop when we stumble; it doesn't waver when we fall. It continues to write, to move, to work in our lives, drawing us closer to Him, redeeming even our worst moments. When we look back on the chapters of our lives, we can see the thread of God's grace woven through it all—the moments when we stumbled, the moments when we felt lost, and the moments when His grace stepped in and wrote a new chapter of love and redemption. And as we continue to walk through life, we can trust that His grace will continue to guide us, to lead us, and to write the story that He has planned for us.

So, even when we stumble, even when we feel like we've fallen too far, we can rest in the truth that God's grace is still at work. It is still writing, still redeeming, still turning our mistakes into something beautiful. God's grace is the pen that writes our story, and it is a story filled with love, with redemption, and with the promise of a new beginning. It is a story that is not defined by our failures but by His faithfulness. And as long as God's grace holds the pen, we can be confident that the story is far from over. There is always another chapter, always another chance, always another moment where God's grace steps in and turns our stumbling into something glorious. And that is the beauty of God's grace—it never gives up on us, never stops writing, and never stops redeeming our lives with His perfect love.

Chapter 3

"With every twist and turn, His grace keeps writing the story we were created for."

With every twist and turn, His grace keeps writing the story we were created for. Life is a journey filled with unexpected detours, moments of joy and sorrow, times of uncertainty, and times of triumph. We often find ourselves in situations that we never imagined, sometimes feeling lost or unsure of where we are headed. But through every single moment, God's grace is at work, shaping our lives and guiding us along the path He has prepared for us. The twists and turns we encounter are not random, nor are they mistakes; they are all part of the grand story God is writing for each of us. A story that, even when we cannot see it, is filled with purpose, love, and redemption. His grace is the unseen hand that gently steers us through the chaos, weaving together the pieces of our lives into something beautiful, something that reflects His glory. The moments of confusion, the seasons of pain, and the unexpected changes are not without meaning—they are the very things that God uses to write the story we were always meant to live.

Every life has its twists and turns, and sometimes they can feel overwhelming. One day, everything seems to be going according to plan, and the next, the road ahead is unclear, and we find ourselves facing challenges we never anticipated. In these moments, it's easy to feel discouraged, to wonder if we've somehow taken the wrong path, or if our lives have gone off course. But the truth is, God's grace is always at work, even when the road seems uncertain. He is not surprised by the detours or the changes in direction—He is the one who sees the entire map of our lives. His grace is what keeps the story moving forward, what turns what we see as mistakes or missteps into opportunities for growth, redemption, and transformation. No twist or turn in our lives is wasted when God's grace is involved. Every experience, no matter how difficult or confusing, is used by Him to write the story He created us for.

God's grace is so much greater than we can ever understand. It is not bound by our limitations, our mistakes, or even our understanding of the path ahead. While we may only be able to see what is right in front of us, God sees the entire journey. He knows where each turn will lead, and He knows exactly how to guide us through the unexpected. What we see as a detour, He sees as a part of His plan. What we see as a failure, He sees as an opportunity for redemption. His grace is not just about picking us up when we fall; it's about continually leading us, shaping us, and preparing us for the life we were created to live. Even when the road ahead seems impossible, even when we feel like we've reached a dead end, God's grace continues to write the story, ensuring that every chapter of our lives brings us closer to the purpose He has for us.

There are times in life when we may feel like the twists and turns are too much to handle. We may question why certain things are happening, why doors are closing, or why the road we thought we were supposed to be on seems to have disappeared. But in those moments, we must remember that God's grace is always at work. He is the Author of our story, and He knows exactly how to navigate every turn. He is never taken by surprise, never caught off guard. His grace is what sustains us, what carries us through the difficult moments and gives us hope for what lies ahead. Even when we don't understand the "why" behind the twists and turns, we can trust that God does. His grace is not only with us in the moments of clarity and joy, but also in the moments of confusion and sorrow. It is in these times, when we are unsure of the path ahead, that His grace becomes our anchor, reminding us that we are never alone, and that our story is still being written with purpose and love.

God's grace is not just about smoothing out the rough patches or making the journey easier. It's about transforming us through every twist and turn. Each moment of our lives, whether it feels like a step forward or a step backward, is part of a larger story—one that God is carefully crafting for our good and His glory. His grace takes the things we would rather avoid—the pain, the failures, the unexpected detours—and uses them to shape us into the people He created us to be. The story of our lives is not one of perfection, but of redemption. It is a story where grace turns every setback into a setup for something greater, where every closed door leads to a new opportunity, and where every painful moment is woven into a beautiful tapestry of God's love and faithfulness.

When we look at the twists and turns of our lives, it can be easy to feel like we've gone off course, like we're no longer on the path we were meant to be on. But God's grace tells us a different story. His grace reminds us that even when we feel lost, we are never truly lost to Him. He knows exactly where we are, and He knows exactly how to lead us forward. Every twist and turn is part of His plan, and His grace is what ensures that we will reach the destination He has for us. The story of our lives is not about avoiding the twists and turns, but about trusting that God's grace is guiding us through them. His grace is what turns the unexpected into the miraculous, what turns the painful into the purposeful.

There is a beautiful freedom that comes from knowing that God's grace is always at work in our lives. We don't have to have all the answers. We don't have to know exactly where the road will lead. We can simply trust that God does. His grace is what writes the story, what takes every twist and turn and uses it for our good. Even when we feel like we've made mistakes, even when we feel like we've taken the wrong path, God's grace steps in and redirects us, ensuring that we are still on the journey He has planned for us. His grace is what turns our confusion into clarity, our doubts into faith, and our fear into courage. It is His grace that writes the story we were created for, and it is His grace that ensures that every chapter, every twist and turn, brings us closer to the purpose He has for our lives.

God's grace is relentless in its pursuit of us. It doesn't stop when the road gets difficult. It doesn't waver when we stumble or fall. It keeps writing, keeps guiding, keeps leading us forward, no matter what. His grace is what sustains us through every twist and turn, what reminds us that our story is not over, even when we feel like we've reached a dead end. The twists and turns of life may seem confusing or overwhelming, but to God, they are all part of His perfect plan. His grace is what turns our confusion into confidence, our fear into faith, and our uncertainty into hope. With every twist and turn, His grace keeps writing the story we were created for, ensuring that we will reach the destination He has for us.

The story of our lives is not one of chaos or randomness. It is a story that is being carefully written by the hand of God, a story that is filled with purpose and meaning. Every twist and turn is part of that story, and God's grace is what keeps it moving forward. His grace is what ensures that no matter what happens, no matter how lost we may feel, we are never outside of His plan. He is always at work, always writing, always guiding us through the twists and turns of life, and leading us closer to the life He has created us to live. His grace is what turns the unexpected into the beautiful, what takes our brokenness and turns it into something whole. With every twist and turn, God's grace keeps writing the story we were created for, and it is a story of love, redemption, and purpose.

So as we navigate the twists and turns of life, let us remember that God's grace is always with us. It is always guiding us, always sustaining us, and always writing the story we were created for. Even when the road ahead seems unclear, even when we don't understand why things are happening the way they are, we can trust that God does. His grace is what ensures that every chapter of our lives is filled with purpose and meaning, and that every twist and turn is leading us closer to the life we were created to live. With every twist and turn, His grace keeps writing the story we were created for, and it is a story that is filled with hope, love, and the promise of a future that is greater than anything we could ever imagine.

Chapter 4

"The ink of grace flows, writing healing where our hearts are broken."

The ink of grace flows, writing healing where our hearts are broken. Imagine a pen held by God Himself, filled with the ink of grace, as it glides across the pages of our lives, writing new chapters of hope, redemption, and healing. We all carry scars, brokenness, and moments where the weight of life feels too heavy to bear. Heartache comes in many forms—whether it's loss, disappointment, betrayal, or simply the deep weariness of carrying burdens for too long. But in the midst of our brokenness, when the cracks in our hearts seem too deep to mend, God's grace enters like a gentle river, flowing steadily, filling every fracture, every wound, and every place that feels shattered beyond repair. His grace doesn't merely cover the brokenness; it transforms it. It works quietly but powerfully, rewriting the pain, turning sorrow into strength, and giving us a new perspective on our suffering. Where there was only despair, God begins to write a story of healing, each stroke of the pen adding light to the darkness and hope to the heaviness of our hearts.

When our hearts are broken, it can feel like nothing will ever be the same. The weight of grief or sadness can make the world seem smaller, darker, and colder. It's easy to believe in those moments that healing is impossible, that the broken pieces of our hearts will never fit back together. We wonder if God sees our pain, if He understands how deep our wounds go. But God does see, and His grace is already at work. It is not a quick fix or a bandage to temporarily cover our wounds; rather, it is a deep, thorough healing that only grace can bring. God's grace doesn't rush the process; it moves with patience and care, taking the time to heal each wound completely. Sometimes, the healing takes longer than we expect, and we may wonder if it will ever come. But even in the moments when we can't see or feel it, the ink of grace is still flowing, still writing healing into the deepest parts of our hearts. It is persistent, relentless in its desire to make us whole again, to restore the broken places and fill them with God's love.

There's something beautiful about the way God uses grace to heal our brokenness. He doesn't ignore the pain or pretend it doesn't exist. Instead, He enters into it with us, meeting us right where we are in the midst of our sorrow. He doesn't offer hollow promises or shallow comfort. He offers Himself—His presence, His love, and His grace. It is in these moments of brokenness that we often feel His grace the most. When we have nothing left to hold on to, when we are at the end of ourselves, God's grace is there, holding us, carrying us through the storm. It writes healing into our story, not by erasing the pain, but by transforming it. The things that once caused us the most pain become the places where God's grace shines the brightest. Our broken hearts become a canvas for God's healing touch, and the ink of grace flows, filling every crack, every void, every empty space.

When we think of healing, we often imagine a quick recovery, a sudden return to how things were before the pain. But the healing that grace brings is different. It doesn't take us back to how things were before; it takes us to something new, something better. The ink of grace doesn't just patch up our broken hearts; it creates something more beautiful in the process. Where there was once brokenness, there is now strength. Where there was once despair, there is now hope. Where there was once emptiness, there is now fullness. God's grace rewrites the story of our lives, using even our most painful moments to create something that reflects His love and His power to heal. The ink of grace flows steadily, patiently, and lovingly, reminding us that no matter how broken we feel, God is not finished with us. He is still writing, still healing, still turning our pain into something glorious.

The world often tells us to hide our brokenness, to put on a brave face, and to pretend that everything is fine, even when it's not. But God invites us to bring our broken hearts to Him, just as they are. He doesn't ask us to hide our pain or to pretend that we're okay. He wants us to come to Him with our wounds, our heartache, and our brokenness, because it is in these places that His grace does its most powerful work. The ink of grace flows freely over our wounds, bringing healing that goes deeper than anything the world could offer. It is not a temporary fix, but a lasting transformation. God doesn't just heal the surface; He heals the root of our pain, reaching into the depths of our hearts and restoring us from the inside out. His grace writes healing into every part of our story, even the parts we thought were beyond repair.

There is something incredibly hopeful about the way God's grace works in our brokenness. It doesn't just heal us; it redeems our pain. The things that once caused us the most hurt become the very things that God uses to show His power and His love. Our broken hearts become testimonies of His grace, stories of how God took what was shattered and made it whole again. The ink of grace flows, not just to heal, but to transform, to make us new. Every scar, every wound, every tear is part of a bigger story—one where God's grace turns our pain into purpose, our sorrow into joy, and our brokenness into beauty.

We may not always understand why we go through seasons of heartache and brokenness. We may wonder why God allows us to experience pain in the first place. But the ink of grace reminds us that God never wastes our pain. He uses it to draw us closer to Him, to show us more of His love, and to make us more like Christ. The healing that comes through grace is not just about making us feel better; it's about making us more like Jesus. It's about shaping us, refining us, and transforming us into the people God created us to be. Our broken hearts are not the end of the story; they are the beginning of something new, something beautiful, something that only God's grace can create.

In those moments when our hearts feel the most broken, when the pain feels unbearable, we can trust that God's grace is at work. Even when we can't see it or feel it, the ink of grace is flowing, writing healing into the deepest parts of our hearts. It is a healing that goes beyond our understanding, a healing that is not rushed but is done with care and love. God's grace is not in a hurry; it takes the time to heal us completely, to make us whole again. The healing may not come in the way we expect or in the timing we want, but it will come, because God's grace never fails. The ink of grace keeps flowing, even when we don't realize it, writing healing into every part of our broken hearts.

The beauty of God's grace is that it meets us in our brokenness and takes us to a place of healing and restoration. It doesn't ignore our pain or minimize our heartache. It enters into it with us, bringing healing that only God can provide. The ink of grace flows through every chapter of our lives, writing a story of redemption, a story of healing, a story of hope. Our broken hearts are not the end of the story; they are the beginning of a new chapter, one where God's grace turns our pain into purpose and our brokenness into beauty. The ink of grace flows, and with every stroke, God writes healing into the story of our lives, reminding us that no matter how broken we feel, we are never beyond the reach of His love.

So if your heart is broken, if you are carrying wounds that feel too deep to heal, know that God's grace is already at work. The ink of grace is flowing, writing healing into every part of your heart. It may take time, it may not happen all at once, but healing is coming. God's grace is persistent, faithful, and powerful. It doesn't stop at the surface; it goes deep, bringing healing that lasts. The ink of grace flows, and it writes healing where our hearts are broken, turning our pain into something beautiful, something that reflects the love and grace of the One who heals us. No matter how broken you feel, God's grace is enough. It is more than enough. It is the very thing that will make you whole again. The ink of grace flows, and with every stroke, it writes healing into your story.

Chapter 5

"Grace is the ink that God uses to rewrite our failures into triumphs."

Grace is the ink that God uses to rewrite our failures into triumphs, and there is something deeply beautiful and transformative about that truth. Life is filled with moments of failure—times when we make mistakes, fall short of our own expectations, or stumble in ways that leave us feeling defeated, ashamed, or lost. It's easy to get caught up in those failures, to believe that they define us, or that they are the end of our story. But with God, failure is never final. Instead, it becomes the very place where His grace steps in and begins to write a new story—one of redemption, growth, and ultimately triumph. Grace isn't a mere covering for our mistakes; it's a powerful force that takes what we thought was ruined and turns it into something better than we could ever have imagined. When we fail, we often feel like we've fallen too far for God to use us again, but grace assures us that God isn't finished with us yet. With each failure, He takes out His pen of grace, dips it in the ink of His love, and begins rewriting our lives in a way that transforms those failures into stepping stones toward victory.

Our failures don't catch God by surprise. He knows every misstep we will take, every mistake we will make, and every time we will fall short. Yet, He chooses to love us anyway, and through His grace, He takes those very moments of failure and rewrites them into stories of triumph. It's not that our failures are ignored or forgotten; rather, they are redeemed. Grace takes the broken pieces of our lives and crafts something new, something better, something that reflects the beauty and strength of God's love. Failure in our eyes might look like the end, but in God's eyes, it's simply the beginning of a new chapter. Each failure is an opportunity for God to display His grace in our lives, to show us and the world that He can take what was meant for harm and turn it into something good. Grace doesn't erase the past; it transforms it. It takes what we once thought was useless and turns it into the very thing that propels us forward into God's plan for our lives.

We all have moments in life where we feel like we've failed beyond repair. Maybe it's a broken relationship, a lost job, a moral failing, or simply the weight of not living up to our own expectations. Those moments can leave us feeling empty, defeated, and wondering if we will ever recover. But God's grace tells a different story. His grace takes those moments of failure and writes over them with words of hope, redemption, and triumph. He doesn't discard us because of our mistakes; instead, He embraces us, offering His grace to rewrite the narrative of our lives. Where we see failure, God sees an opportunity for His grace to shine. He uses the ink of grace to take our worst moments and turn them into the very things that lead us to our greatest victories. It's not that He minimizes our failures, but rather, He shows us that they do not have the final say. Grace is what turns our failures into triumphs, what takes the ashes of our mistakes and makes something beautiful out of them.

The beauty of grace is that it meets us right where we are, in the midst of our failures. We don't have to clean ourselves up or fix everything on our own before coming to God. His grace meets us in our mess, in our brokenness, and in our failure. It is His grace that does the work of transformation. When we bring our failures to God, He doesn't condemn us or hold our mistakes over us. Instead, He takes His pen of grace and begins rewriting the story. What we thought was over, He shows us is just the beginning. Grace is what empowers us to move forward, to learn from our mistakes, and to grow into the people God created us to be. Failure doesn't disqualify us from God's love or His plans for us. In fact, it's often in our failures that we experience His grace the most powerfully. It's in those moments of brokenness that God's grace picks us up, dusts us off, and sets us on a path toward victory.

Failure is a part of life, but it doesn't have to define us. God's grace ensures that our failures are not the end of the story. Instead, they become part of the story that God is writing in our lives—one where grace takes our mistakes and uses them to create something even more beautiful. Grace is not just about forgiving us for our failures; it's about transforming those failures into something that brings glory to God and good to us. Every time we fail, grace steps in to remind us that we are not alone, that God is with us, and that He is still working in our lives. The ink of grace flows over every mistake, every misstep, and every failure, rewriting them into stories of triumph. God doesn't just give us second chances; He gives us new beginnings. With every failure, grace offers us the opportunity to start again, to move forward, and to become who God has called us to be.

One of the most beautiful things about grace is that it doesn't just fix what's broken—it makes it better. God doesn't just put a bandage over our failures and hope for the best. No, He takes those failures and turns them into victories. He takes the very things that we thought would destroy us and uses them to strengthen us, to grow us, and to show us His love in a deeper way. Grace takes the wounds of our failures and turns them into marks of His faithfulness. Our failures become testimonies of His grace, stories of how God took what was broken and made it whole again. When we look back on our lives, we will see that the moments of failure were not the end, but the very moments where God's grace stepped in and began writing a new chapter—one of victory, growth, and triumph.

God's grace is relentless. It doesn't give up on us, even when we feel like giving up on ourselves. When we fail, grace is already at work, rewriting the story, turning our failures into the very things that lead us to triumph. We may stumble, we may fall, but God's grace is always there to pick us up, to write a new chapter, and to remind us that our failures are not the end. Grace tells us that we are more than our mistakes. It tells us that we are loved, forgiven, and still part of God's plan. It tells us that failure is not the end of the story, but the beginning of something new and beautiful. Grace turns our failures into triumphs by taking what was meant for harm and using it for good, by taking what was broken and making it whole again.

The ink of grace never runs dry. It keeps flowing, keeps writing, and keeps transforming. No matter how many times we fail, no matter how big the mistakes we've made, God's grace is always enough to rewrite the story. It is always enough to turn our failures into triumphs. Grace is the ink that God uses to take the broken pieces of our lives and turn them into something beautiful. It is the ink that writes hope where there was despair, peace where there was chaos, and victory where there was defeat. Grace doesn't erase the past; it redeems it. It takes every failure and turns it into a stepping stone toward the future that God has planned for us.

In the hands of God, our failures are never wasted. They become the very places where His grace does its most powerful work. Where we see failure, God sees potential. Where we see defeat, God sees the opportunity for victory. Grace is what bridges the gap between our failures and God's triumph. It is what takes our mistakes and turns them into the very things that lead us closer to Him. God's grace is not just about forgiveness; it's about transformation. It's about taking what was broken and making it whole, taking what was lost and bringing it back, and taking what was a failure and turning it into a triumph.

So when we fail, when we fall short, when we make mistakes, we don't have to live in shame or defeat. We can bring our failures to God, knowing that His grace is already at work, rewriting the story. We can trust that no failure is too big for God's grace, no mistake is beyond His ability to redeem. Grace is the ink that God uses to rewrite our failures into triumphs, and as long as God holds the pen, the story is not over. It is a story of hope, of redemption, and of victory—a story where grace turns every failure into a triumph.

Chapter 6

"Even when we lose our way, God's grace draws the map for our return."

Even when we lose our way, God's grace draws the map for our return. Life is often like a journey, full of winding paths, unexpected detours, and stretches of road that seem to lead nowhere. Along the way, we sometimes stumble, wander off course, or find ourselves completely lost, not knowing how to get back to the place where we belong. It can be frightening to realize that we've strayed from the path, that the light that once guided us now feels dim or distant, and that we don't know how to make our way back. Yet, in these moments of confusion, fear, and disorientation, God's grace steps in. It is not a distant force that waits for us to figure it all out on our own. No, God's grace is active, loving, and personal, and even when we are most lost, His grace is already at work, gently, persistently drawing the map that will lead us back to Him. His grace is like the light at the end of a tunnel, like a compass pointing true north, showing us that no matter how far we've wandered, no matter how tangled the path may seem, there is always a way back to His love, His peace, and His purpose for our lives.

There are moments in life when we feel as though we've completely lost our way. Maybe it's a result of poor choices, or perhaps we've simply drifted, not intentionally turning away from God, but still finding ourselves far from where we should be. The distractions of the world, the pressures of daily life, and even our own desires can pull us off course, until one day we wake up and realize we are no longer walking the path God set before us. In those moments, it's easy to feel shame, guilt, and despair. We may wonder how we could have strayed so far, or we might even doubt whether we can ever return to the place we once were. But the beauty of God's grace is that it meets us right where we are. We don't have to find our own way back, because God is already reaching out to us, already drawing the map that will lead us back into His arms.

God's grace is like the guiding hand of a loving Father. Even when we are too lost to know where to begin, He never leaves us to wander aimlessly. His grace is a map that patiently draws us back, step by step, toward the life we were meant to live. It doesn't matter how many wrong turns we've taken, or how far we've drifted. God's grace can reach us wherever we are. It's like a divine GPS that never loses track of our location, always recalculating, always finding a way to guide us back to the path He intended for us. When we lose our way, grace doesn't abandon us or give up on us. Instead, it marks a new path forward, one that leads us out of the wilderness and back into the safety of God's plan.

Sometimes, the hardest part of losing our way is feeling like we are beyond help, like we've fallen too far or strayed too far off the path for anyone to find us. But the truth is, we are never too lost for God. His grace is infinite and all-encompassing. No matter how far we've wandered, no matter how many times we've lost our way, God is always with us, gently calling us back, drawing us closer to Him. His grace is relentless in its pursuit of us. It doesn't matter if we've taken one wrong turn or a thousand; God's grace never stops working to bring us back into His presence. He is like the good shepherd who leaves the ninety-nine to find the one lost sheep. Even when we are far from Him, He is near to us, searching for us, calling us, and drawing the map that will guide us back to His love.

One of the most comforting truths about God's grace is that it doesn't just wait for us to figure out how to return. It doesn't stand at a distance, watching as we struggle to find our way back. Instead, grace comes to us, meets us where we are, and walks with us every step of the way. When we are too weak to take another step, when the path ahead seems too confusing or too overwhelming, God's grace carries us. It shows us the way, one step at a time, leading us gently but surely back to the place where we belong. Even when we've lost sight of God, He never loses sight of us. His grace draws the map, showing us that no matter how lost we feel, we are never truly lost to Him.

Grace is not just a map that shows us the way back; it is the very means by which we return. God doesn't just point us in the right direction and leave us to find our own way. No, His grace actively leads us, guides us, and empowers us to take each step. It is by grace that we find our way back to God, and it is by grace that we are welcomed home. There is no condemnation in God's grace. When we return, we are not met with judgment or anger. We are met with open arms, with the love of a Father who has been waiting for His child to come home. Just like the prodigal son, we may expect to be treated as less than we were, to be met with disappointment for having lost our way, but instead, we find a celebration, a warm welcome, and the restoration of everything we thought we had lost. That is the power of grace.

Even when we lose our way, God's grace draws the map for our return, but it doesn't stop there. It also heals the wounds we've acquired along the way. When we wander, we often get hurt. We may stumble, fall, and carry the scars of our journey. But grace doesn't just bring us back to God; it heals us in the process. It restores what was broken, binds up our wounds, and makes us whole again. The journey back to God is not just about finding our way; it's about being made new, about experiencing the full power of God's grace to heal, restore, and transform. Grace doesn't just show us the way back—it walks with us, heals us, and makes us better than we were before.

There is no place we can go that is too far for God's grace to reach. We may lose our way in the darkness, but God's grace is the light that shines through, illuminating the path back to Him. We may feel lost in a wilderness of our own making, but God's grace is the map that leads us through the wilderness and back to His presence. There is no wrong turn, no mistake, no sin that can separate us from the love of God, because His grace is always greater. It is always enough. Even when we lose our way, God's grace never loses us. He is always there, always drawing the map, always showing us that we are loved, that we are wanted, and that we have a place with Him.

God's grace is patient. It doesn't rush us or force us back onto the path. It gently guides us, giving us the time we need to turn around, to find our footing, and to start walking in the right direction. Grace is not harsh or demanding. It is kind, tender, and understanding. God knows that we will lose our way from time to time, and He is not angry with us for it. Instead, He is compassionate, always ready to guide us back, always ready to show us the way home. His grace is like a steady hand on our shoulder, gently steering us in the right direction, reminding us that we are never alone on this journey.

Even when we lose our way, God's grace is the constant that never changes. It is the one thing we can always count on, the one thing that will always lead us back to where we need to be. It is not dependent on our ability to find our own way; it is entirely dependent on God's love for us. And that love is unchanging, unwavering, and unconditional. No matter how many times we lose our way, God's grace is always there, drawing the map for our return, leading us back to the life He has for us. Grace is what brings us home.

In the end, we may lose our way a thousand times, but God's grace will always bring us back. It is the map that never fails, the guide that never loses sight of us, and the force that will always lead us back to the heart of God. No matter how far we've wandered, no matter how lost we feel, God's grace is enough. It is more than enough. It will always draw the map for our return, and it will always lead us home. Even when we lose our way, God's grace is there, guiding us, restoring us, and bringing us back to the place where we belong—in His arms, in His love, and in His perfect plan for our lives.

Chapter 7

"In the hands of grace, every tear we shed becomes part of a beautiful new chapter."

In the hands of grace, every tear we shed becomes part of a beautiful new chapter. Life, with all its unpredictable twists and turns, often brings moments of sorrow, pain, and heartbreak. At times, it feels as though the tears we shed come from a well that never runs dry, as if the pain is too deep, too overwhelming to be healed. In these moments, it's easy to feel as though our tears are wasted, as though they're simply a sign of our brokenness, our weakness, or the emptiness we feel. But in the hands of God's grace, our tears are not wasted. Each tear is seen, each tear is counted, and each tear holds meaning. God, in His infinite love and mercy, takes those very tears—the ones that we think are a sign of our failure or despair—and uses them to write something new, something beautiful. Grace takes our sorrow and shapes it into something transformative, turning what feels like the end of our story into the beginning of a new chapter, one that reflects His power to heal, restore, and bring hope even in the darkest of circumstances.

When we cry, it can feel like the world is closing in around us, like the weight of our burdens is too much to bear. Whether we are crying from loss, disappointment, fear, or pain, those tears can make us feel isolated and alone, as though no one else could possibly understand the depth of our hurt. But God does. He sees each tear that falls, and in His grace, He promises that not a single one is in vain. Psalm 56:8 tells us that God collects our tears in His bottle, a beautiful image that reminds us that our tears matter to Him. They are not forgotten or overlooked. Instead, God takes those tears, and in the hands of grace, He transforms them. What was once a sign of brokenness becomes a sign of renewal, of God's unfailing love working in our lives even when we can't see it or feel it. Every tear we shed becomes part of a story of redemption, a story that only grace can write.

Grace has a way of turning even our deepest sorrows into opportunities for growth and healing. It doesn't ignore or minimize our pain. Instead, it meets us in the very depths of our sadness and begins to write something new. When we cry, we may feel as though we are at our weakest, but in those moments, God's grace is at its strongest. It is in our moments of greatest need that grace shines brightest, taking the tears we shed and using them to water the seeds of hope, peace, and joy that will bloom in the next chapter of our lives. We may not be able to see that new chapter as we cry, but God, in His infinite wisdom and love, is already writing it. He is already turning the page, already working to bring beauty from our ashes and joy from our mourning.

There are seasons in life when the tears seem endless. We face hardships that feel too great to overcome, losses that feel too painful to bear. We may wonder why God allows us to go through such difficult times, why He doesn't simply take away the pain and stop the tears from falling. But the truth is, God is always with us in our sorrow. He never leaves us alone in our pain. Instead, His grace surrounds us, comforting us, holding us, and reminding us that even in our darkest moments, He is still at work. In the hands of grace, our tears are not a sign of defeat, but a sign that God is preparing us for something greater. He is using those tears to soften our hearts, to deepen our faith, and to remind us of His presence even in the midst of our pain.

Every tear we shed becomes part of the tapestry that God is weaving in our lives. Each one is a thread that, when woven together with His grace, creates something beautiful, something that reflects His love and His faithfulness. We may not understand why we have to cry, why we have to go through certain trials, but we can trust that God is always working for our good. In Romans 8:28, we are reminded that all things work together for good for those who love God and are called according to His purpose. This means that even our tears—those moments when we feel most broken—are being used by God to bring about something beautiful in our lives. Grace takes those tears and weaves them into a story of hope, of redemption, and of new beginnings.

There is a beauty in knowing that God is not distant from our pain. He is not a God who watches us cry from afar, but a God who draws near to us in our sorrow, who collects our tears and holds them in His hands. In those moments when we feel most vulnerable, when the tears flow freely and we can't seem to stop them, God is already at work. His grace is already turning those tears into the ink that will write the next chapter of our lives, a chapter filled with healing, peace, and joy. We may not see it right away, but we can trust that grace is always writing, always working, always turning our pain into something that will glorify Him and strengthen us.

Sometimes, we may feel like we are crying over the same things, over and over again. The same heartaches, the same disappointments, the same struggles. We may wonder if we will ever stop crying, if the pain will ever end. But grace reminds us that there is a purpose to every tear. Each one is part of the process of healing, part of the journey that will eventually lead us to a place of peace and joy. God's grace is patient with us, allowing us to cry, allowing us to grieve, but never leaving us in that place of sorrow. Instead, He uses those tears to cleanse our hearts, to prepare us for the new things He is doing in our lives. In the hands of grace, every tear is a tool that God uses to bring us closer to Him, to teach us more about His love, and to shape us into the people He created us to be.

The tears we shed may feel like they are falling into the void, like they are lost in the wind, but in reality, they are falling into the hands of God, where they are held, cherished, and transformed by His grace. No tear is wasted. Every tear we cry becomes part of the story that God is writing in our lives, a story that is filled with His grace and His love. In those moments when we are crying, when the pain feels overwhelming, we can take comfort in knowing that God is already at work, writing the next chapter of our story. And in that chapter, we will see the beauty that comes from the pain, the joy that comes from the sorrow, and the triumph that comes from the tears.

God's grace has a way of turning what feels like an ending into a new beginning. When we cry, we may feel like it's the end, like there's no way forward, no hope for healing or redemption. But grace steps in and says, "This is not the end. This is just the beginning." In the hands of grace, our tears become the foundation for a new chapter, one where God's love and power are on full display. The tears we shed today are not the end of our story; they are the ink that God uses to write something new, something beautiful, something that reflects His glory and His goodness.

We may not always understand why we have to cry, why we have to go through certain trials and hardships. But we can trust that God's grace is always at work, even in the midst of our pain. He is always writing, always turning the page, always drawing us closer to Him. Every tear we shed becomes part of the story that He is writing in our lives, a story that is filled with grace, hope, and redemption. In the hands of grace, every tear is transformed into something beautiful, something that glorifies God and brings us closer to the purpose He has for our lives.

In the end, our tears are not a sign of weakness or failure. They are a sign that we are human, that we feel deeply, and that we are in need of God's grace. And in His hands, those tears become part of a beautiful new chapter, one where healing is found, where joy is restored, and where God's love is evident in every part of our lives. So even when the tears flow, even when the pain feels overwhelming, we can trust that God's grace is at work, writing a story of redemption, a story where every tear becomes part of something beautiful and new. In the hands of grace, every tear we shed is part of a story that leads to hope, healing, and a deeper understanding of God's love.

Chapter 8

"His grace rewrites the lines of doubt and fear into courage and faith."

His grace rewrites the lines of doubt and fear into courage and faith, and it's in those very moments of our deepest uncertainty and trembling that God's grace begins its most transformative work. When we stand on the edge of life's hardest challenges—when we face the unknown, when the future is unclear, or when fear grips our hearts—it's easy to let doubt whisper lies that we are not enough, that we don't have the strength to make it through, or that God is distant and unconcerned with our struggles. But in these moments, God's grace gently takes the pen and begins to rewrite the narrative that fear and doubt have tried to script over our lives. Where once the lines of our story were filled with hesitation and insecurity, grace intervenes and fills those spaces with words of hope, strength, and faith. It's not a loud or sudden rewriting, but rather a steady, patient, and powerful transformation, turning our moments of greatest fear into opportunities for courage and growth. It is grace that silences the voice of doubt and ushers in a renewed sense of confidence in who God is and who He has created us to be. In the face of our fears, God's grace tells a new story—one where we are not defined by our uncertainties but by His unwavering love and strength, where courage rises in the very places where fear once held us captive.

Doubt often sneaks into our hearts quietly, sometimes without us even realizing it. It shows up in our inner thoughts when we question our worth, our purpose, or even God's plans for our lives. We may wonder if we're really enough, if we can handle what lies ahead, or if God will come through for us as He has promised. Fear, too, is a close companion of doubt, filling our hearts with the paralyzing sense that things may go wrong or that we're not equipped to face the challenges before us. But this is where God's grace steps in. His grace doesn't just brush aside our doubts or ignore our fears—it addresses them directly. Grace is like a soothing balm, applied to the wounds of our hearts, healing the places where doubt and fear have taken root. It gently but firmly begins to rewrite the lines, erasing the lies of doubt and replacing them with the truth of God's promises. Grace reminds us that it is not about our ability or strength, but about God's power working through us. It is grace that gives us the courage to face the unknown, to walk in faith even when the path ahead is uncertain.

When fear tries to tell us that we're alone, that no one understands the battles we're facing, grace speaks a different word. Grace tells us that God is always with us, that He sees every fear, every tear, every worry, and that He is working even in the moments when we feel most afraid. His grace is like a light that pierces through the darkest clouds of fear, reminding us that we are never truly alone. In those moments when doubt whispers that we can't possibly move forward, grace gives us the strength to take one more step, to keep going, knowing that we are held by the One who holds the entire universe in His hands. God's grace rewrites our fear-filled story, showing us that courage is not the absence of fear, but the decision to trust God in the midst of it. It is grace that transforms our shaky steps into bold strides, leading us to places we never thought we could go, empowering us to face challenges we never imagined we could conquer.

Doubt has a way of distorting our view of God's plans for us. It makes us question whether we're really on the right path, whether God's promises are really true, or whether we are capable of fulfilling the purpose He has for our lives. But grace rewrites those lines of doubt with faith. Faith that God's plans for us are good, even when we don't fully understand them. Faith that He is faithful to every promise He has made. Faith that, in His timing, all things will work together for our good, as Romans 8:28 so beautifully reminds us. Grace turns our doubt into a deeper trust in God's sovereignty and His perfect plan for our lives. Even when we can't see the full picture, grace gives us the faith to believe that God is working behind the scenes, that He is orchestrating every detail for His glory and our good. In the hands of grace, our doubt is not a stumbling block but a stepping stone that leads us into a deeper, more profound faith.

Fear can be so overwhelming at times that it feels like a wall we cannot climb over. It paralyzes us, holds us back, and makes us feel powerless. But grace is the force that breaks through that wall, rewriting the lines of fear into courage. It is grace that gives us the boldness to stand in the face of fear and declare that God is greater than anything we may face. Grace empowers us to walk through the valley of the shadow of death, knowing that God's rod and staff are there to comfort and protect us, as Psalm 23 reminds us. It is grace that turns our moments of trembling into moments of triumph, where we realize that fear doesn't have the final word—God's grace does. His grace is what enables us to rise above the fears that threaten to overwhelm us, to trust that He is with us every step of the way, and to know that His strength is made perfect in our weakness, just as 2 Corinthians 12:9 promises.

Courage is not something we muster up on our own. It is a gift of grace. When we feel too weak, too uncertain, too afraid to move forward, grace steps in and fills the gaps. It gives us the courage we never thought we had, the strength we didn't know we possessed, because it is God working through us. Grace reminds us that we are not walking this journey alone. We are being led by the One who has already overcome every obstacle, who has already won every battle, and who promises to be with us always, even to the end of the age. In the hands of grace, our fears become opportunities for God to display His power and glory in our lives. What we once saw as insurmountable challenges become moments where God's grace carries us through, teaching us to rely not on our own understanding, but on His wisdom and guidance.

Faith is not about having all the answers. It's about trusting the One who does. And grace is what allows us to have that faith, even when everything around us seems uncertain. When doubt tries to cloud our vision, grace clears the way, helping us to see beyond the temporary struggles and into the eternal truth of God's promises. Grace gives us the faith to believe that God is for us, that He is with us, and that nothing can separate us from His love. It is grace that rewrites the story of doubt, showing us that faith is not about never questioning, but about trusting God even in the questions. It's about believing that He is bigger than our doubts, greater than our fears, and that His plans for us are far better than anything we could imagine.

God's grace doesn't just rewrite the lines of doubt and fear—it transforms them. It turns the very things that once held us back into the things that propel us forward. Our doubts become the places where we learn to trust God more deeply. Our fears become the spaces where God's strength is made perfect in our weakness. Grace is not just a gentle correction; it is a radical transformation. It takes what was once broken and makes it whole. It takes what was once fearful and makes it courageous. It takes what was once filled with doubt and fills it with faith. In the hands of grace, our lives are continually being rewritten, transformed from fear into faith, from doubt into trust, from uncertainty into boldness.

Even in our moments of greatest doubt and fear, God's grace is always at work, rewriting the story. It is grace that takes the broken pieces of our hearts and mends them with courage. It is grace that takes our shaky faith and builds it into something strong and unshakable. And as grace continues to rewrite the lines of our lives, we begin to see that what once seemed like insurmountable obstacles were actually opportunities for God to show His power and love. We begin to see that our doubts were the very things that led us to a deeper faith, and that our fears were the very places where God's courage took root.

In the end, it is grace that transforms everything. It is grace that rewrites the lines of doubt and fear, turning them into a story of courage, faith, and victory. And as long as God's grace holds the pen, we can be confident that the story He is writing is one of hope, one of strength, and one where His love always wins. Even when we feel overwhelmed by doubt and fear, we can trust that God's grace is already at work, rewriting the lines, turning the page, and leading us into a future filled with courage, faith, and the undeniable presence of His love.

Chapter 9

"The pen of grace never runs dry, even when our hope feels empty."

THE PEN OF GRACE NEVER runs dry, even when our hope feels empty. Life can sometimes feel overwhelming, like a vast ocean of uncertainty that pulls us under, leaving us gasping for breath. We face seasons where it seems like everything we hoped for has slipped through our fingers, and we wonder if we will ever find the strength to hold on again. Whether it's the loss of a dream, the weight of disappointment, or the burden of waiting for something that seems so far off, hope can feel like a flickering flame that is about to go out. In those moments of darkness, when the future seems uncertain and the present feels too heavy to bear, we can start to believe that God's grace, like our hope, has run dry. But the incredible truth is that God's grace is never exhausted. It is never limited by our circumstances or our feelings. Even when we feel like we have nothing left, when our hearts are weary and our hope feels empty, God's grace is still flowing, still writing, still at work. The pen of grace never stops. It moves steadily, faithfully, and powerfully across the pages of our lives, filling the emptiness with renewed hope, with a story of redemption, and with the unwavering love of the One who holds our lives in His hands.

Hope is such a fragile thing. It's easy to hold onto when life is going well, when the sun is shining, and everything seems to be falling into place. But when storms come, when life throws us unexpected challenges, or when we find ourselves in seasons of waiting, hope can begin to fade. We start to wonder if things will ever get better, if the promises God made will ever come to pass, or if we've somehow been forgotten. Our hearts feel heavy, our minds are filled with doubt, and the future seems like an empty page with nothing written on it. But in these moments of despair, when hope seems like a distant memory,

God's grace is still writing. The pen of grace never runs dry, even when our hope does. Grace is not dependent on our feelings or our circumstances. It doesn't waver when we waver. It doesn't grow weak when we grow tired. God's grace is constant, steady, and relentless. It keeps moving, keeps writing, keeps filling our lives with hope, even when we don't see it.

There are times in life when we feel like we've reached the end of our strength, when we've prayed every prayer, cried every tear, and still find ourselves in the same difficult place. We may wonder if God's grace has run out for us, if we've somehow used up all the chances, all the mercy, all the hope that He had to give. But the truth is, God's grace is infinite. It never runs out. It never runs dry. His grace is like a river that never stops flowing, always moving, always refreshing, always renewing. Even when we can't see it or feel it, God's grace is still at work. It is still writing the story of our lives, still filling the empty places with hope, with promise, and with the assurance that God is not finished with us yet. The pen of grace continues to write, even when we feel like the page is blank, even when we can't imagine how things will get better, or when we feel like giving up. Grace is the force that keeps our story moving forward, even when we feel stuck.

Hope and grace are intimately connected. It is grace that fuels our hope, that reminds us that no matter how dark things seem, there is always light ahead. Grace tells us that God is always working, always moving, even in the silence, even in the waiting, even in the moments when we feel most alone. The pen of grace never runs dry because God never stops being faithful. He never stops caring for us, never stops writing the story He has planned for our lives. Grace is what carries us through the hardest seasons, the moments when we feel like we have nothing left to give, when our faith feels weak, and our hope feels like it's slipping away. Grace steps in and reminds us that God's promises are true, that His love is unchanging, and that His plans for us are still good. Even when our hope feels empty, God's grace is overflowing, abundant, and more than enough to sustain us.

The beauty of grace is that it meets us right where we are. It doesn't wait for us to have everything figured out or to feel full of hope and faith. Grace meets us in our emptiness, in our brokenness, in our doubt, and in our fear. It meets us in the moments when we feel like we have nothing left to hold onto, when the weight of life feels too heavy to bear. And in those moments, grace doesn't just give us a little bit of hope—it floods our hearts with the assurance that God is with us, that He is for us, and that He is working all things together for our good. The pen of grace never stops writing, never stops filling the pages of our lives with the goodness of God's love. Even when we feel like the story has stalled, like we've reached a dead end, grace is already writing the next chapter, a chapter filled with hope, with promise, and with new beginnings.

It's easy to feel like we've come to the end of our story when things aren't going the way we planned. When the job falls through, when the relationship ends, when the diagnosis is worse than we imagined, hope can feel like it's slipping away. We may feel like the page is blank, like our future is uncertain, and like we don't know what to do next. But the truth is, God's grace is still writing. The pen of grace never runs dry, even when our hope does. God is still at work, even in the moments when we can't see it. He is still writing our story, still filling the empty places with His love, His peace, and His promise that He will never leave us or forsake us. Grace is what keeps us going when we feel like we can't take another step. It's what gives us the strength to keep moving forward, even when the path ahead is unclear. Grace reminds us that God is still in control, that He is still writing our story, and that His plans for us are still good.

When our hope feels empty, grace steps in and fills the gaps. It fills the spaces where doubt has crept in, where fear has taken hold, and where we feel like we're not enough. Grace reminds us that we don't have to have all the answers, that we don't have to have everything figured out. All we need to do is trust in the One who holds the pen, the One who is writing our story with love, with purpose, and with grace. God's grace is what turns our empty hope into something new, something beautiful, something that reflects His glory and His goodness. The pen of grace never runs dry because God's love for us never runs out. He is always with us, always working, always writing the story of our lives, even when we can't see it or feel it.

There are moments in life when we feel like we've been waiting forever, when the promise seems so far off, and hope feels like it's fading. We may wonder if God has forgotten us, if He's still writing our story, or if we've somehow missed our chance. But grace reminds us that God is always working, always moving, always writing. Even in the waiting, even in the silence, God is at work. The pen of grace never stops moving, never stops writing, never stops filling the pages of our lives with hope, with promise, and with His unfailing love. Grace gives us the strength to keep hoping, to keep believing, to keep trusting that God is still in control, that He is still writing our story, and that His plans for us are still good.

God's grace is more than just a gentle comfort in our time of need—it is a powerful force that transforms our lives, that takes our empty hope and fills it with His promises. Grace is what turns our despair into hope, our fear into faith, and our emptiness into fullness. It is grace that reminds us that God's love for us is unchanging, that His plans for us are still good, and that He is still writing the story of our lives. The pen of grace never runs dry because God's love for us never ends. He is always with us, always writing, always filling the pages of our lives with His goodness, His mercy, and His love.

Even when our hope feels empty, even when the future seems uncertain, we can trust that God's grace is still at work. The pen of grace is still writing, still filling the pages of our lives with His promises, His love, and His purpose. Grace is what carries us through the hardest seasons, the moments when we feel like we have nothing left to give, when our hope feels like it's fading. It is grace that reminds us that God is still in control, that He is still writing our story, and that His plans for us are still good. The pen of grace never runs dry, even when our hope does, because God's love for us is unending, and His promises are true.

Chapter 10

"Each page of our story is touched by grace, even when the words feel heavy."

Each page of our story is touched by grace, even when the words feel heavy. Life is a journey filled with moments that sometimes seem too overwhelming to endure. There are days when the weight of our burdens feels like too much, when the struggles we face seem endless, and the pain we carry in our hearts threatens to overshadow every trace of joy. It's during these moments that we find ourselves feeling lost, broken, or even defeated, as if the chapters of our lives are written in ink too dark to ever see through. The words of disappointment, heartache, fear, and uncertainty seem to fill the pages, and we wonder how we will ever find the strength to turn the next page. Yet, even in the midst of this heaviness, even when the words of our story feel too painful to bear, God's grace is at work. His grace touches each page of our lives, filling even the darkest moments with hope, love, and redemption. God's grace does not ignore the heaviness, but it enters into it, transforming it, reminding us that every chapter, no matter how difficult, is part of a greater story that He is writing for our good and His glory.

When the words of our story are heavy with sorrow, it can be hard to see how grace is present in those moments. We may question where God is when life feels unbearable, when the weight of our circumstances makes it difficult to even breathe. But God's grace is not absent during our most trying times. In fact, it is during these times that His grace is most powerful. It may not come in the way we expect, but grace is always there, holding us, sustaining us, and carrying us through the pain. Grace is the soft whisper in the silence of our suffering, the gentle reminder that we are not alone, even when the world feels like it is crashing down around us. It is the assurance that God is still writing our story, even when the words feel like too much to bear. His grace fills the spaces between the lines, turning our pain into purpose and our sorrow into strength.

The words of our lives are not always filled with joy and light. There are times when the pages are marked by deep grief, loss, and fear. But grace has a way of turning even those heaviest moments into something beautiful. It doesn't erase the pain or pretend that it doesn't exist. Instead, grace takes that pain and weaves it into the fabric of our story, using it to create something meaningful, something that reflects God's power to heal and restore. Each tear we cry, each heartache we endure, is touched by God's grace. He is not distant from our suffering; He is present in it, walking with us through the valley of the shadow of death, as Psalm 23 reminds us. His grace is what gives us the strength to keep going, to turn the next page, even when we feel like we can't.

When the words of our story feel heavy with fear, it is grace that rewrites those lines, turning fear into faith. Fear can paralyze us, make us feel like we are trapped in a never-ending cycle of anxiety and doubt. But God's grace steps in and reminds us that we are not defined by our fear. We are defined by His love, His mercy, and His faithfulness. Grace gives us the courage to move forward, even when we are scared, to trust in God's plan, even when we don't understand it. It is grace that takes the heaviest words of fear and transforms them into a story of hope and trust in the One who holds our future in His hands. Each page of our story, even the ones filled with fear, is touched by grace, turning our doubt into belief and our worry into peace.

There are seasons in life when the words of our story feel heavy with uncertainty. We don't know what lies ahead, and the unknown can be terrifying. We may feel lost, unsure of the path we're on, and wonder if we're even headed in the right direction. But God's grace meets us in those moments of uncertainty. It is grace that reassures us that even when we don't know what's coming next, God does. He knows the beginning and the end of our story, and He is guiding us every step of the way. His grace is what allows us to trust in Him, even when we can't see the full picture. It is grace that gives us the peace to rest in the knowledge that God is in control, that He is writing our story with purpose, and that He is working all things together for our good, just as Romans 8:28 reminds us. Even when the words of our story are filled with uncertainty, grace touches those pages and fills them with the assurance of God's unfailing love and His perfect plan.

When the words of our story feel heavy with loss, it is grace that holds us in the midst of our grief. Loss can leave us feeling empty, as if a piece of our heart has been torn away, and we may wonder how we will ever move forward. But God's grace is present in our loss. It is the comfort that comes in the quiet moments, the peace that surpasses all understanding, as Philippians 4:7 tells us. Grace doesn't take away the pain of our loss, but it gives us the strength to keep living, to keep loving, and to keep believing that there is still beauty to be found, even in the midst of our brokenness. Grace fills the empty spaces left by loss, reminding us that God is near to the brokenhearted, that He heals our wounds, and that He is with us in our sorrow. Each page of our story, even the ones marked by loss, is touched by grace, turning our mourning into hope and our grief into a deeper understanding of God's love.

The words of our story are not always what we expect. There are times when life takes an unexpected turn, when our plans fall apart, and we are left wondering what comes next. But grace is what carries us through the detours. It is grace that reminds us that God's plans are higher than our plans, that His ways are higher than our ways, as Isaiah 55:8-9 tells us. Grace allows us to let go of our own expectations and trust that God is writing a better story than we could ever imagine. Even when the words of our story don't make sense to us, grace is at work, turning what we see as setbacks into opportunities for growth and transformation. Each page of our story, even the ones filled with unexpected twists and turns, is touched by grace, leading us closer to God's purpose for our lives.

When the words of our story feel heavy with regret, grace steps in and rewrites the narrative. We all make mistakes, we all have moments we wish we could take back, but grace reminds us that we are not defined by our past. We are defined by God's love and His forgiveness. Grace takes the heavy words of regret and replaces them with words of redemption. It is grace that allows us to move forward, to learn from our mistakes, and to grow into the people God has called us to be. Each page of our story, even the ones filled with regret, is touched by grace, turning our failures into testimonies of God's mercy and His power to redeem.

The words of our story are often written in the midst of the unknown. We don't know what tomorrow holds, and that uncertainty can weigh heavily on our hearts. But grace is what gives us the peace to live in the present, to trust in God's timing, and to believe that He is in control of the future. Grace reminds us that we don't have to have all the answers, that we don't have to know what's coming next, because God does. Each page of our story, even the ones filled with uncertainty, is touched by grace, filling our hearts with peace and our minds with the assurance that God is always at work, even when we can't see it.

Grace is the thread that runs through every page of our story, connecting the moments of joy with the moments of sorrow, the moments of clarity with the moments of confusion, and the moments of strength with the moments of weakness. It is grace that gives us the strength to keep going, to keep believing, and to keep trusting that God is writing a story of redemption, hope, and love. Even when the words of our story feel heavy, even when the burdens we carry seem too much to bear, grace is always there, holding us, sustaining us, and reminding us that we are never alone.

God's grace is the constant in our ever-changing lives. It is the anchor that holds us steady in the storms, the light that guides us in the darkness, and the hope that carries us through the hardest times. Each page of our story is touched by grace, even when the words feel heavy, because God is always with us, always working, always writing a story that is filled with His love, His mercy, and His redemption. No matter what we face, no matter how heavy the words of our story may feel, we can trust that God's grace is more than enough. It is the grace that carries us, the grace that sustains us, and the grace that turns our heaviest moments into testimonies of His faithfulness and His love.

Chapter 11

"When life scribbles chaos, grace rewrites peace and purpose."

When life scribbles chaos, grace rewrites peace and purpose, and this beautiful truth shines brightest in the darkest, most confusing moments of our lives. Life has a way of throwing us into the whirlwind, tossing us into storms we never saw coming, and pulling us into a state of confusion where nothing seems to make sense. One minute, everything feels calm and clear, and the next, we are surrounded by chaos—unexpected tragedies, heartbreak, financial strain, health crises, broken relationships, and dashed dreams. The world can seem like a place that spins out of control, scribbling messes across the pages of our lives, leaving us bewildered and wondering what happened to the plans we had so carefully made. In those moments, it feels like everything is unraveling, like the order we had once held onto is slipping through our fingers, and we are left grasping at the fragments, trying to make sense of the madness. But it's in these very moments that grace steps in. Where we see chaos, God sees an opportunity for grace to rewrite the story. Where we see confusion, He sees the space to bring peace. Where we feel lost and without purpose, grace reorders the pieces of our lives, bringing divine purpose out of what we thought was just disorder. Chaos may scribble its mess across the pages of our lives, but God's grace holds the pen that rewrites it all into something meaningful, something filled with peace, something overflowing with purpose.

Life's chaos can be overwhelming, like a tidal wave that crashes over us, threatening to sweep us away in its current. We try to hold on, to regain control, to fix the mess that seems to be growing by the minute, but no matter how hard we try, the more tangled and chaotic things become. We start to wonder where God is in all of it. Has He left us to deal with this mess on our own? Is He still present in the midst of the confusion? But grace reminds us that God is never far. Even in the midst of chaos, He is close, and His grace is already at work, rewriting the story in ways we cannot yet see. He is not the author of chaos, but He is the author of peace. And it's His grace that takes the scribbles of chaos and disorder and gently begins to reshape them, turning the confusion into clarity, turning the noise into stillness, and bringing peace where there once was only turbulence. Grace is not a loud force that shouts over the chaos; rather, it is a quiet but powerful presence that settles in, calming the storm, and reminding us that even in the chaos, God is still in control.

In moments of chaos, it's easy to lose sight of the bigger picture. The immediate storm can feel so consuming that it blocks out any hope of seeing beyond it. The challenges we face, the uncertainties that keep us awake at night, and the fears that grip our hearts seem to be the only things that exist in that moment. But grace has a way of gently lifting our eyes above the storm, above the scribbled mess that life has thrown at us, and showing us the bigger picture—God's picture. Grace reminds us that no matter how chaotic life seems, God is still writing the story. And He is writing it with peace and purpose. He has a plan, a purpose for every moment, even the ones that feel disordered and messy. Grace whispers to us that this chaos is not the end, that there is something greater being worked out, something beautiful that God is shaping from the broken pieces. What we see as chaos, God sees as a canvas for His peace and purpose to be displayed.

The world around us often feels like it's scribbling chaos into every part of our lives. From the pressures of work and school to the expectations of family and society, the demands can feel overwhelming, like a constant scribble of noise that never quiets down. We feel pulled in every direction, trying to juggle responsibilities, trying to meet everyone's expectations, trying to hold it all together. But in the midst of the scribbled chaos, grace comes in like a breath of fresh air, clearing the clutter, silencing the noise, and bringing us back to a place of peace. Grace doesn't just tidy up the mess; it transforms it. It takes the scribbles and rewrites them into something that reflects God's peace—a peace that surpasses all understanding, as Philippians 4:7 promises us. This peace is not dependent on our circumstances being perfect or everything going according to plan. It's a peace that comes from knowing that, even in the chaos, God is with us, that He is working all things together for good, and that His grace is more than enough to carry us through.

But grace doesn't stop at bringing peace; it goes further, bringing purpose into the very chaos that once seemed meaningless. When life scribbles chaos, we can feel as though our sense of direction and purpose has been completely lost. We may wonder why certain things are happening, why our plans are falling apart, or why the path ahead seems so unclear. It can feel like we're wandering in the dark, unsure of which way to go or how to make sense of the mess we're in. But grace doesn't leave us in the dark. Grace is like a light that illuminates the path, showing us that even in the midst of chaos, there is purpose. God's purpose is not lost in the scribbles. He is still at work, still weaving every moment—both the beautiful and the chaotic—into a greater plan for our lives. Grace shows us that what we see as random scribbles are actually part of a much bigger picture, one that God is carefully crafting with love and intention.

Purpose is something we all crave, something we all search for, especially in times of chaos. We want to know that the mess we're going through isn't for nothing, that there's a reason behind it, that something good can come out of it. And this is exactly what grace promises us. Grace reminds us that nothing in our lives is wasted—not a single tear, not a single moment of confusion, not a single storm. God uses it all. He takes the chaos, the scribbles that seem to have no order or meaning, and He rewrites them into a story of purpose. The very things that we thought were random and pointless become the places where God's grace shines the brightest, where His purpose is revealed most clearly. Grace transforms the chaos into something that brings glory to God and deepens our understanding of who He is.

When life scribbles chaos, it's easy to feel out of control, like everything is spiraling beyond our ability to manage. But grace reminds us that we were never meant to be the ones in control. God is the One who holds the pen. He is the One who is writing the story, and His grace ensures that no matter how chaotic things may seem, He is still guiding the narrative. Grace reassures us that even when we don't understand what's happening, even when the chaos feels overwhelming, God is still in control, and His purpose will prevail. His plans are good, even when we can't see them, and His grace is sufficient, even when we feel weak.

In times of chaos, grace becomes our anchor. It holds us steady when the waves of life are crashing around us, when everything seems uncertain and out of place. Grace is what keeps us grounded in the truth that God is faithful, that He is with us, and that He is working all things together for our good. Grace is what allows us to find peace in the midst of the storm, to trust that God is not only present in the chaos but that He is actively working to bring about His purpose through it.

And in this, grace is not just a force that rewrites the chaos—it is a reminder of who God is. Grace tells us that God is not distant or disconnected from our struggles. He is near. He is present in the mess, in the scribbles of chaos, and He is at work, bringing peace where there was once confusion, bringing purpose where there was once disorder. Grace is the constant assurance that, no matter what life throws our way, God's love for us is unchanging, His plans for us are good, and His grace is sufficient to see us through.

As life continues to scribble its chaos across the pages of our lives, grace will always be there to rewrite the story, to bring peace in the midst of the storm, and to reveal the purpose that God has woven into every moment. We may not always understand why things happen the way they do, but we can trust that God's grace is always at work, taking the chaos and turning it into something beautiful, something meaningful, something filled with His peace and His purpose.

So when life feels like a chaotic mess, when the scribbles seem to have no rhyme or reason, remember that grace is still writing. God is still in control, and He is using every moment of chaos to shape something far greater than we can imagine. His grace will always rewrite peace and purpose into the story of our lives, no matter how messy the scribbles may be. And as long as grace holds the pen, we can trust that the story is far from over.

Chapter 12

"In the book of our lives, grace highlights every lesson and underlines every blessing."

In the book of our lives, grace highlights every lesson and underlines every blessing. From the moment we take our first breath, each of us begins writing a story—a story that will be filled with joys, sorrows, challenges, triumphs, and countless unexpected twists and turns. Life is not a straight, simple path; it is a winding journey, filled with highs and lows, moments of clarity and times of confusion. We walk through seasons of abundance, where blessings seem to overflow, and we walk through seasons of drought, where it feels as though everything has been stripped away. But through it all, whether in moments of triumph or moments of trial, one thing remains constant: God's grace. His grace is woven into every chapter, into every moment of our lives. It is the hand that gently guides us, the light that illuminates our path, and the steady force that shapes us, grows us, and teaches us the lessons we need to learn. Grace doesn't just touch the pages of our lives—it highlights every lesson and underlines every blessing, ensuring that nothing is overlooked, nothing is wasted, and nothing is forgotten in the grand story God is writing for us.

There are times in life when the lessons we need to learn are hard, when the trials we face seem overwhelming, and we wonder why we are going through such difficulties. In these moments, it can be easy to feel frustrated, to question God's plan, or to wonder if He is still with us. But grace is always at work, even in the most difficult seasons of our lives. Grace doesn't erase the challenges or pretend that they don't exist; instead, it highlights the lessons we need to learn through them. It teaches us patience when we are in seasons of waiting, endurance when the road ahead seems long and unending, and trust when we can't see the way forward. Grace takes the moments of struggle and turns them into opportunities for growth. It opens our eyes to the deeper truths that God is teaching us, even when we are in the midst of pain or uncertainty. It reminds us that every lesson we learn, every struggle we endure, is shaping us into the people God has called us to be. Grace highlights these lessons, ensuring that we don't miss the wisdom that is hidden in our challenges, that we don't overlook the growth that is taking place in our hearts, even when life feels hard.

But grace doesn't just highlight the hard lessons—it also underlines every blessing, big or small, that God pours into our lives. In a world that is often filled with noise, chaos, and distractions, it can be easy to overlook the blessings that are right in front of us. We can become so focused on the things we don't have, on the prayers that seem unanswered, or on the dreams that feel far out of reach, that we fail to see the many ways God is blessing us every single day. But grace steps in and reminds us to slow down, to open our eyes, and to see the blessings that are all around us. It underlines those moments of joy, of love, of provision, and of peace, making sure that we don't miss the gifts that God is giving us, even in the most ordinary moments. Grace shows us that every breath we take, every sunrise we witness, every friendship we cherish, every act of kindness we receive is a blessing from God. It opens our hearts to gratitude, reminding us that even when life feels difficult, there is still so much to be thankful for.

When we look back on the story of our lives, we can see the fingerprints of grace on every page. There are moments we thought would break us, but grace stepped in and gave us the strength to keep going. There are times when we felt lost, unsure of where to turn, but grace gently guided us back onto the right path. There are chapters of our lives that were filled with heartache, but grace was there, holding us, comforting us, and reminding us that we were not alone. Grace has been present in every lesson we've learned, whether it was a lesson about faith, about forgiveness, about perseverance, or about love. Grace has been the thread that has woven our story together, ensuring that every chapter, every moment, has a purpose and a meaning.

And then there are the blessings—the moments of pure joy, of answered prayers, of unexpected gifts that remind us of God's goodness and faithfulness. Grace underlines these blessings, making sure that we don't forget them, that we don't take them for granted. It helps us to remember that every good thing in our lives is a gift from God, that His love for us is unending, and that His provision for us is constant. Grace underlines the moments of laughter, the moments of peace, the moments of connection with others, and the moments when we feel the warmth of God's presence. It ensures that we hold onto these blessings, that we carry them with us through the difficult times, and that we allow them to strengthen our faith and deepen our trust in God's goodness.

In the book of our lives, grace is not just a passive presence—it is an active force, shaping every chapter, guiding every decision, and transforming every situation. It highlights the lessons that are most important for us to learn, ensuring that we grow in wisdom, in faith, and in love. It underlines every blessing, making sure that we never lose sight of the goodness and faithfulness of God, even when life feels hard. Grace is the lens through which we are able to see the deeper meaning in our struggles and the abundant blessings in our lives. It teaches us to trust in God's plan, even when we don't understand it, and to be grateful for the many ways He is working in our lives, even when we can't see it.

There are times when the lessons we need to learn come through pain, through loss, or through disappointment. But grace is always there, highlighting the lessons that will make us stronger, that will deepen our faith, and that will draw us closer to God. It is grace that helps us to see that even in our struggles, God is working for our good, that He is teaching us something important, something that will shape the rest of our lives. Grace helps us to see that every lesson, no matter how difficult, is a step toward becoming the people God created us to be. It highlights the moments of growth, the moments of transformation, and the moments when we learn to trust in God more fully. Grace ensures that we don't miss the lessons that are most important, that we don't overlook the ways God is shaping us, even in the hardest times.

And when life is filled with blessings—when our prayers are answered, when our dreams come true, when we experience the fullness of God's provision—grace underlines those moments, ensuring that we don't forget them. It reminds us to stop and give thanks, to recognize that every good thing in our lives comes from God, and to see His hand at work in every detail. Grace helps us to see the beauty in the ordinary, the gifts in the everyday moments, and the blessings that we might otherwise overlook. It underlines the moments of joy, of love, of peace, and of gratitude, reminding us that God is always with us, that He is always providing for us, and that His love for us is unchanging.

In the book of our lives, grace is the constant that runs through every page, every chapter, every moment. It is the hand that highlights the lessons we need to learn, ensuring that we grow in wisdom and faith. It is the pen that underlines every blessing, reminding us of God's goodness, His faithfulness, and His love. Grace is what makes sense of our story, what gives meaning to the struggles and the joys, the lessons and the blessings. It is the thread that weaves everything together, creating a beautiful tapestry of God's love and His plan for our lives.

When we look back on the story of our lives, we will see the many ways that grace has been at work. We will see the lessons that have shaped us, the blessings that have sustained us, and the love that has carried us through every moment. Grace will be the highlight on every page, underlining the moments of joy, of growth, and of faith, reminding us that God has been with us every step of the way, guiding us, teaching us, and blessing us. And as we continue to write the story of our lives, we can trust that grace will continue to be with us, highlighting every lesson, underlining every blessing, and ensuring that our story is one of faith, hope, and love.

Chapter 13

"God's grace is the pen that never forgets to include the beauty in our brokenness."

God's grace is the pen that never forgets to include the beauty in our brokenness. This truth is a profound reminder that, in the story of our lives, no moment of pain, failure, or heartache is ever wasted. We often try to hide our brokenness, believing that the shattered parts of our hearts or the mistakes we've made are things we need to cover up or erase. We convince ourselves that only the perfect parts of our story are worthy of being told, that only our strengths and successes are the moments that matter. But God's grace tells a different story. It tells us that even in our weakest moments, even when we feel like we are falling apart, there is beauty. God's grace does not overlook our brokenness—it sees it, acknowledges it, and redeems it. It is with the pen of grace that God writes our story, and He never forgets to include the beauty that emerges from the very places where we feel most broken. It is in these places of vulnerability, failure, and hurt that grace shines the brightest, turning our shattered pieces into a masterpiece, revealing the beauty that only God's hand can create.

In the world, brokenness is often seen as something to be ashamed of. We are taught to put on a brave face, to pretend that we have it all together, and to hide the parts of ourselves that are cracked, flawed, or damaged. We are conditioned to believe that only the perfect, the whole, and the strong are valuable. But God's perspective is so different from the world's. He doesn't turn away from our brokenness; instead, He draws near to it. He isn't repelled by our wounds; He moves closer to heal them. And in the process, He reveals a kind of beauty that could never have been seen without the brokenness. Grace is the pen that writes this story, and it is a pen that never skips over the hard parts, the painful parts, the parts that we wish weren't there. Instead, grace leans into those moments and turns them into something more beautiful than we ever could have imagined. It is through our brokenness that God's strength is made perfect, as 2 Corinthians 12:9 reminds us, and it is through His grace that beauty is born from even the deepest pain.

There is something incredibly comforting about the fact that God's grace doesn't erase our brokenness but transforms it. When we are in the midst of our pain, whether it's the result of loss, failure, or the struggles of life, it can feel like nothing good could ever come from it. The weight of our brokenness can be so overwhelming that it blinds us to the possibility of beauty or redemption. We may feel like the shattered pieces of our hearts and lives are beyond repair, too far gone for anything good to emerge. But that's where grace steps in. Grace doesn't simply patch up the broken places; it takes those very pieces and uses them to create something new. It is in the cracks, in the brokenness, that God's grace pours in, filling the empty spaces with His love, His mercy, and His healing. And as His grace works, it brings out the beauty that we never could have seen on our own. It's a beauty that isn't diminished by the fact that we were broken; in fact, it's a beauty that is made even more radiant because of it.

The pen of grace is always at work, writing a story that includes every part of who we are—the good, the bad, the broken, and the redeemed. Grace doesn't leave out the hard chapters; it doesn't skip over the times when we've fallen, failed, or been hurt. Instead, it incorporates those moments into the bigger picture of God's plan for our lives. What we often see as the ugliest parts of our story—our brokenness, our mistakes, our weaknesses—are the very places where God's grace does its most beautiful work. It is through grace that God rewrites the narrative of our brokenness, turning it into a testimony of His love, His power, and His ability to redeem even the most shattered lives. In God's hands, our brokenness is not a mark of shame; it is the canvas on which His grace paints something beautiful.

One of the most incredible aspects of God's grace is that it doesn't require us to be whole before we come to Him. We don't have to fix ourselves or pretend that we aren't broken in order to receive His grace. In fact, it is often in our moments of greatest brokenness that we experience God's grace the most powerfully. When we come to Him with our shattered hearts, with the pieces of our lives that feel too broken to mend, He welcomes us with open arms. His grace is not reserved for the perfect or the put-together. It is for the broken, the weary, the lost, and the hurting. And in His grace, He takes our broken pieces and begins to create something new. He doesn't discard us because we are broken; instead, He uses our brokenness as part of His masterpiece. It is through His grace that beauty emerges from our pain, and it is through His love that we are made whole.

We often try to hide our brokenness, afraid that it makes us less worthy of love or less valuable in God's eyes. But grace tells us that our brokenness is not something to be ashamed of. It is a part of our story, and it is a part that God is actively working in. Grace doesn't just tolerate our brokenness—it transforms it. It takes the cracks in our hearts and fills them with God's love, creating a new kind of beauty that could never have existed without the brokenness. When we allow God's grace to work in our lives, we begin to see that our brokenness is not the end of the story. It is the beginning of something new, something beautiful, something that reflects God's glory in a way that only our unique story can.

God's grace is the pen that never forgets to include the beauty in our brokenness because it is through our brokenness that His grace shines the brightest. It is in our moments of greatest need that we experience the fullness of His love and mercy. When we are at our weakest, when we feel like we have nothing left to give, grace steps in and carries us. It lifts us up, it heals us, and it shows us that we are not defined by our brokenness, but by God's love for us. In the hands of grace, our brokenness becomes a vessel through which God's power is displayed. It becomes a testimony of His ability to take what was broken and make it whole again. And in the process, we begin to see the beauty that was there all along, hidden beneath the surface, waiting for grace to bring it to light.

The beauty that comes from brokenness is not a superficial beauty. It is a deep, lasting beauty that comes from knowing that we are loved by a God who doesn't shy away from our mess but enters into it with us. It is a beauty that comes from seeing how God's grace has taken the very things we thought would destroy us and used them to build something stronger, something more beautiful, than we ever could have imagined. It is a beauty that is born out of the knowledge that God's grace is always at work, even in the darkest, most broken places of our lives. And it is a beauty that reminds us that no matter how broken we feel, we are never beyond the reach of God's grace.

God's grace is the pen that writes the story of our lives, and it never forgets to include the beauty in our brokenness because that is where His grace does its most transformative work. It is in the places where we feel most fragile, most wounded, and most lost that God's grace steps in and begins to write a new story. A story of healing, of redemption, of beauty rising from the ashes. Grace doesn't erase our brokenness; it redeems it. It takes the very things that we thought would be our undoing and turns them into the foundation of something beautiful, something that reflects the goodness and faithfulness of God.

When we look back on the story of our lives, we will see the fingerprints of grace all over it. We will see how God took our broken pieces and made something beautiful out of them. We will see how His grace was always at work, even in the moments when we felt most lost, most broken, and most afraid. And we will see that, in the hands of grace, our brokenness was never something to be ashamed of. It was the place where God's love met us most deeply, where His power was made perfect in our weakness, and where His grace turned our story into something beautiful.

God's grace is the pen that never forgets to include the beauty in our brokenness, and as long as His grace is writing our story, we can trust that our brokenness is not the end. It is the beginning of something new, something beautiful, and something filled with the love and grace of the One who never stops writing. In the hands of grace, our brokenness is transformed into beauty, and our story becomes a testimony of the incredible, redeeming power of God's love.

Chapter 14

"The story may feel unfinished, but grace is still crafting the perfect ending."

The story may feel unfinished, but grace is still crafting the perfect ending. In life, there are countless moments when we feel as though our story is incomplete, as if the final chapter hasn't been written and the loose ends of our hopes, dreams, and struggles are left hanging in uncertainty. We find ourselves in seasons where nothing makes sense, where the weight of unanswered prayers, unfulfilled expectations, and ongoing struggles presses down on us, and we wonder if God has forgotten the conclusion to our tale. We may look around at the broken pieces of our lives and feel that the journey has stalled, that the promises once held so dear are now distant, and that the dreams we carried in our hearts are now only faint echoes. It's in these moments that we need the reminder that God's grace is not done with us yet. His grace is still moving, still weaving, still writing, still crafting, even when we can't see it. Though the story may feel unfinished, we can rest assured that grace is at work, shaping every moment—both the joys and the pains—into a beautiful ending that only God, the ultimate Author, can create.

So often in life, we want to rush toward the resolution. We long for the happy ending, for the moment when everything finally makes sense, when the pieces of our story come together in a way that brings closure, satisfaction, and peace. We desire clarity, the resolution to our struggles, the fulfillment of our longings. But life doesn't always unfold the way we expect or on the timeline we desire. Sometimes, we find ourselves stuck in the middle of a chapter that feels endless, a chapter filled with pain, confusion, or uncertainty. The road ahead is clouded, the path behind feels like a string of failures, and the present feels like a battle we're losing. It is in these moments of unfinished stories that God's grace steps in, reminding us that the ending has not yet been written, and that it is His grace that holds the pen. Grace whispers to us that the current chapter is not the final word, that even though we cannot see the full picture, God is still at work, writing a story of redemption, healing, and purpose.

There is something beautiful about the way God works in the unfinished parts of our lives. He is not hurried by our impatience, nor is He overwhelmed by the messiness of our story. Where we see confusion and uncertainty, God sees opportunity for His grace to shine. He takes the broken, incomplete pieces of our lives and begins to craft something new, something far more beautiful than we could ever imagine. His grace is not bound by time or by our limited understanding. It moves steadily, quietly, and powerfully, shaping our lives in ways that only God can. Even when we feel like nothing is happening, when it seems as though we've been forgotten or left in the waiting, grace is still working, still writing. Every moment, every tear, every struggle is being used by God to craft a perfect ending that reflects His goodness, His love, and His purpose for our lives.

We often forget that life is a process, and that God is not just interested in the destination, but in the journey. Grace is not just about the final chapter; it is present in every page, every line, every word of our story. It is present in the moments of joy, and it is present in the moments of sorrow. It is there when we feel strong, and it is there when we feel weak. Grace meets us where we are, in the unfinished parts of our lives, and reminds us that God's work is not yet complete. Philippians 1:6 tells us that "He who began a good work in you will carry it on to completion until the day of Christ Jesus." This means that God is not done with us yet. The story may feel unfinished, but grace is still crafting, still shaping, still molding us into the people He created us to be.

The idea of an unfinished story can be unsettling, especially when we face moments in life that don't make sense. When we experience heartbreak, loss, failure, or disappointment, it's easy to feel like we're stuck in a chapter we never wanted to live through. We wonder why God hasn't answered our prayers, why the healing hasn't come, why the doors haven't opened, or why the pain continues. But grace reminds us that the story is not over yet. The current chapter, no matter how difficult, is not the final one. God's grace is still at work, still crafting the perfect ending, and it is in these very moments of struggle that His grace is most powerfully at work. Grace is not a passive force that sits by while we struggle; it is an active force that moves into the very heart of our pain, rewriting the narrative of our lives with hope, healing, and redemption.

We may not always understand the twists and turns in our story. There will be times when the road ahead is unclear, when we face obstacles that seem insurmountable, and when we are left questioning what God is doing. But even in the midst of the uncertainty, grace assures us that God is still in control. He is still writing our story, and He is working all things together for good (Romans 8:28). The chapters that feel unfinished, the ones that leave us with more questions than answers, are often the very places where God's grace is most powerfully at work, shaping us, growing us, and preparing us for the future He has planned. Grace turns our doubts into trust, our fears into courage, and our pain into purpose. It reminds us that we don't have to have all the answers, because God does, and He is crafting a story that is far greater than anything we could write on our own.

The beauty of grace is that it doesn't require us to have everything figured out. We don't have to know how the story will end in order to trust that God is writing something beautiful. Grace meets us in our uncertainty, in our confusion, and in our doubt, and it reminds us that we are not the ones responsible for crafting the perfect ending—God is. His grace carries us through the unfinished parts of our lives, giving us the strength to keep moving forward, even when we don't see the whole picture. Grace gives us the faith to trust that God is good, even when the road is hard, and that His plans for us are still good, even when life doesn't go the way we expected.

When we look at the unfinished parts of our story, it's easy to feel discouraged. We see the mistakes we've made, the dreams that have fallen apart, the unanswered prayers, and the struggles we've faced, and we wonder how anything good could come from it all. But grace reminds us that God is not finished with us yet. He is still crafting, still writing, still shaping our lives into something beautiful. What we see as unfinished, God sees as an opportunity for His grace to shine. The very places where we feel most broken, most lost, and most uncertain are the places where God's grace is working the hardest, crafting a story that will reflect His glory and His love.

The perfect ending that grace is crafting may not look like what we expect. It may not come in the way we planned or on the timeline we imagined. But we can trust that God's grace is always at work, and that the ending He is crafting is far better than anything we could have written ourselves. Grace doesn't erase the struggles or the pain; instead, it transforms them into something meaningful, something beautiful. It takes the unfinished parts of our story and weaves them into a tapestry of redemption, healing, and hope. It is through grace that God turns our ashes into beauty, our mourning into joy, and our sorrow into dancing (Isaiah 61:3). The story may feel unfinished, but grace assures us that God is still at work, and that the final chapter will be one of victory, of restoration, and of His unfailing love.

As we walk through the unfinished parts of our story, we can rest in the knowledge that grace is always enough. It is enough to carry us through the uncertainty, enough to sustain us in the waiting, and enough to bring us to the perfect ending that God has planned. Grace gives us the strength to keep going, to keep believing, and to keep trusting that God is faithful, even when we can't see the whole picture. The story may feel unfinished, but grace reminds us that God is still writing, and that the ending He is crafting will be far more beautiful, more redemptive, and more full of purpose than we could ever imagine.

In the end, grace teaches us that the unfinished parts of our story are not a sign of failure, but a sign that God is still at work. He is not done with us yet. He is still shaping, still refining, still crafting the perfect ending that will reflect His love and His grace. And as long as God's grace holds the pen, we can trust that our story is far from over, and that the best is yet to come. The story may feel unfinished, but grace is still crafting the perfect ending, and we can rest in the assurance that God's plans for us are always good, always full of hope, and always filled with His unchanging love.

Chapter 15

"Even in the margins of our mistakes, God's grace writes hope and healing."

Even in the margins of our mistakes, God's grace writes hope and healing. Life is a journey filled with choices, and sometimes, despite our best intentions, we stumble. We make decisions that we later regret, take paths we wish we hadn't, or fall into behaviors and habits that hurt ourselves and those around us. We fail to live up to our own expectations, and at times, we feel like we've fallen so far that there's no way back. The weight of guilt can press heavily on our hearts, and the sting of regret can seem like it will never fade. We look at the mistakes we've made—big and small—and wonder if our story is now irreparably marred by the ink of our failures. But even in those margins, where the lines of our lives seem scribbled with error, God's grace enters. His grace doesn't ignore our mistakes, nor does it condone them. Instead, it redeems them, transforming the very places where we feel the most broken, lost, or ashamed into places of profound hope and healing. Grace is the pen that God uses to write a new story in the very places where we thought our story had been ruined, and it is there, in those margins, that God writes His most beautiful words of restoration.

Mistakes are a part of the human experience, and no one is immune to them. We try our best to navigate life, but we inevitably fall short. Perhaps we've said things in anger that we wish we could take back, or maybe we've hurt someone we love through our actions or inactions. There are times when we may feel like we've completely derailed our lives, and the guilt that follows can feel suffocating. But God's grace is not limited by our mistakes. Where we see only failure, God sees an opportunity for growth, for redemption, for healing. His grace steps into the mess we've made and gently begins to rewrite the narrative. He takes the very mistakes that we thought would define us and uses them to reveal His love, His mercy, and His power to restore. In the margins of our failures, God's grace writes words of forgiveness, reminding us that we are not defined by our worst moments, but by His unchanging love for us.

God's grace is always present, even when we feel furthest from Him. When we make mistakes, it's easy to believe the lie that we are too far gone for grace to reach us. We convince ourselves that we need to clean up our act before we can return to God, that we must somehow fix the mess we've made before He will welcome us back. But the truth is, God's grace is already there, waiting for us, even in the midst of our mistakes. His grace is not something we earn by being good enough or by fixing our failures. It is a gift, freely given, even when we feel least deserving of it. Grace meets us in the very moments when we feel most unworthy, and it begins the process of healing our hearts and restoring our lives. In the margins of our mistakes, God's grace doesn't just cover them up; it transforms them. It turns our failures into opportunities for deeper faith, for greater reliance on Him, and for a renewed sense of purpose.

There's a powerful truth in the fact that God's grace is most evident in our weaknesses. In the moments when we feel like we've messed up beyond repair, when the weight of our mistakes feels too heavy to bear, God's grace steps in and reminds us that we are not alone. He is with us, even in the midst of our failure. His grace doesn't come with condemnation or judgment; it comes with open arms, offering us hope for a new beginning. It is in the margins of our mistakes, in the very places where we feel most broken, that God writes a new story—one of healing, one of restoration, one of hope. He takes the ink of our errors and rewrites them with His love, turning what we saw as an ending into a new chapter filled with grace.

The beauty of grace is that it doesn't erase our mistakes, but it redeems them. God doesn't pretend that our failures never happened. Instead, He takes those very failures and uses them to shape us, to teach us, and to draw us closer to Him. In the margins of our mistakes, God's grace writes hope by reminding us that our story is not over. The mistakes we've made do not define us, and they do not have the final say. Grace tells us that no matter how far we've fallen, no matter how badly we've messed up, there is always hope for healing and restoration. God's grace is bigger than our mistakes, and it has the power to turn even the darkest moments of our lives into testimonies of His goodness and His love.

It's easy to feel overwhelmed by guilt when we make mistakes. We replay the moments over and over in our minds, wondering how we could have done things differently, wishing we could go back and make a better choice. But God's grace invites us to stop dwelling on the past and to focus on the future that He is crafting for us. Grace doesn't just offer us a second chance; it offers us a fresh start, a new beginning, a new chapter in our lives where the mistakes of the past are transformed into opportunities for growth. In the margins of our mistakes, God's grace writes healing by showing us that we are not beyond redemption. He heals the wounds we've caused, both in ourselves and in others, and He restores what was broken. Grace is the bridge that takes us from guilt to forgiveness, from shame to healing, from brokenness to wholeness.

There is a deep comfort in knowing that God's grace is not conditional. It is not based on how well we perform or how perfectly we live our lives. It is a gift that is given freely, even when we feel most undeserving of it. In the margins of our mistakes, when we feel like we've failed too many times to count, God's grace is still there, offering us hope, offering us healing, offering us a way forward. His grace doesn't just patch up the mistakes we've made; it transforms them into something beautiful. It turns the places where we feel most lost into the very places where we find God's love in the most powerful way. It is in our mistakes, in our failures, that God's grace shines brightest, reminding us that we are loved, forgiven, and never beyond the reach of His mercy.

God's grace is the ultimate healer. It heals the wounds we've inflicted on ourselves through poor choices, and it heals the wounds we've caused in others. It brings restoration where there was once brokenness, and it brings peace where there was once turmoil. In the margins of our mistakes, God's grace writes a new story, one that is filled with hope and healing. It takes the mess we've made and turns it into a message of redemption. It shows us that even when we feel like we've messed up beyond repair, God is still at work, crafting something beautiful out of the broken pieces of our lives. His grace is always enough, always sufficient, always present, even in the moments when we feel most undeserving of it.

One of the most powerful aspects of God's grace is that it doesn't leave us where it finds us. Grace doesn't just forgive us for our mistakes; it transforms us. It changes our hearts, renews our minds, and gives us the strength to move forward in a new direction. In the margins of our mistakes, God's grace writes hope by reminding us that we don't have to stay stuck in our failures. We don't have to be defined by the mistakes we've made. Grace offers us a way out, a way forward, a way to live a new life that is filled with purpose, with hope, and with the knowledge that we are loved by a God who never gives up on us.

Even in the margins of our mistakes, God's grace is always writing, always redeeming, always offering us hope and healing. No mistake is too big for God's grace, no failure too great for His love. He takes the places where we've fallen, the places where we've made wrong choices, and He turns them into places of restoration. Grace is the pen that God uses to rewrite our story, and in the margins of our mistakes, He writes words of hope, of healing, of new beginnings. Our mistakes are not the end of the story; they are the place where God's grace begins to work in the most powerful way, transforming our failures into testimonies of His love and His mercy.

In the end, it is God's grace that defines us, not our mistakes. It is His love, His forgiveness, and His mercy that shape the story of our lives. Even in the margins of our mistakes, God is at work, writing a story of hope and healing that reflects His goodness and His faithfulness. Our mistakes may be part of our story, but they are not the whole story. Grace ensures that the final word in our lives is one of redemption, one of restoration, and one of hope. And as long as God's grace holds the pen, we can trust that no mistake is beyond repair, no failure is beyond redemption, and no story is beyond the reach of His love.

Chapter 16

"God's pen of grace turns every 'no' into 'not yet' and every 'failure' into 'future.'"

God's pen of grace turns every "no" into "not yet" and every "failure" into "future." Life is filled with moments when we are faced with closed doors, missed opportunities, and what feel like absolute dead ends. We have dreams that seem to fall apart, prayers that seem to go unanswered, and hopes that appear to dissolve into nothing. In those moments, it's easy to feel like the story of our lives is being written in failure, rejection, and disappointment. We ask God for things, and when the answer seems to be "no," it can feel like our plans have been ruined and our future derailed. But in those very moments, God's grace steps in and reminds us that what looks like a definitive "no" from our limited perspective is often simply a "not yet" in God's perfect plan. Grace rewrites the story in ways we could never have anticipated, taking what seems like the end and transforming it into a delay that carries purpose. When we see closed doors, God sees the perfect timing. When we feel stuck in the frustration of waiting, grace whispers that the waiting itself is not wasted. Every "no" is not the end—it is a redirection, a pause that prepares us for something better, something more aligned with God's will for our lives. And what feels like failure is not the final chapter; it is the beginning of a future that only God, with His infinite wisdom, can craft.

We often struggle with the "no's" in life. We pray for healing, for provision, for relationships to be restored, for doors to open, and when those prayers seem to go unanswered, or the answer is "no," we're left feeling confused and hurt. We wonder why God, who loves us so much, would deny us something we believe is good. We question whether we're being punished or whether we're somehow unworthy of the blessings we're asking for. But God's grace reassures us that His "no" is never a rejection, and it is never the end of the story. Instead, it's His way of saying, "Not yet. Trust Me. I'm still working." Grace shifts our perspective from disappointment to trust, teaching us that God's timing is always perfect, even when it doesn't match our expectations. It reminds us that just because something hasn't happened yet doesn't mean it will never happen. God's "not yet" is filled with purpose, even when we don't understand it. He sees the whole picture—the things we cannot see from our limited viewpoint—and He knows exactly when and how to bring about the answers we seek in ways that will truly fulfill us, in ways that align with His perfect plan for our lives.

In the waiting, God's grace does its most transformative work. The times when we are forced to wait for answers, for breakthroughs, for dreams to come to fruition are often the times when God is preparing us for what's ahead. Grace takes the moments of frustration, of uncertainty, of seemingly unanswered prayers, and turns them into seasons of growth. It is in the waiting that God molds us, shapes our character, deepens our faith, and teaches us to rely fully on Him. While we are focused on the "not yet," God is focused on our heart, on the lessons we need to learn, on the strength we need to gain, and on the preparation that is necessary for the next chapter of our lives. His grace reminds us that the waiting is not punishment—it's preparation. It's a time when God is working behind the scenes, orchestrating things we cannot see, and getting us ready for the future He has planned. And when that future arrives, we will be able to look back and see that every "not yet" was a necessary step toward something greater than we could have imagined.

Failure, too, is something we all face at some point in life. We make plans that fall apart, we take risks that don't pay off, we pursue dreams that seem to crumble in our hands. Failure can feel like a final verdict, like a label that defines us and limits our future. It's easy to feel like our failures disqualify us from God's blessings or from the future we once hoped for. But grace steps in and rewrites the narrative. Grace takes every failure and transforms it into a future. Where we see only loss, grace sees opportunity for growth, for learning, for refining. God doesn't see our failures as the end of the story; He sees them as part of the process. Grace takes the broken pieces of our failures and uses them to build something stronger, something more beautiful, something that reflects God's ability to redeem even the most shattered dreams. What we see as failure, God sees as a stepping stone toward the future He has planned for us.

God's grace doesn't erase our failures; it redeems them. Every failure we experience is an opportunity for God to show us His power, His love, and

His ability to turn things around in ways we never expected. Failure humbles us, reminds us of our need for God, and often redirects us onto a path that is better than the one we were pursuing. It is in the moments of failure that we are reminded that our worth is not based on our achievements, but on God's love for us. Grace takes our failures and transforms them into future victories. It turns the things we thought were dead ends into new beginnings. It shows us that no failure is too great for God to use, and that even when we feel like we've reached the end of the road, God is already crafting a new path, a new future, filled with His purpose and His promise.

The beauty of grace is that it never lets our failures have the final say. Where we see failure, grace sees potential. Where we see a door that has closed, grace sees a window that is about to open. Where we see the end of a dream, grace sees the beginning of something even better. God's grace is not limited by our failures; in fact, it thrives in them. It is in the moments when we feel most defeated, most broken, most lost that God's grace shows up in the most powerful way. Grace takes the ashes of our failures and turns them into something beautiful, something that glorifies God and points to His redemptive power.

God's pen of grace turns every "no" into "not yet" and every "failure" into "future" because He is always at work, even when we can't see it. His plans for us are good, and His grace is always sufficient to carry us through the waiting, through the disappointment, and through the failures. What we see as setbacks are often setups for something greater. What we see as closed doors are often God's way of protecting us from something that isn't right for us or preparing us for something that is even better. Grace reminds us that God's "no" is never a rejection—it is a redirection. It is His way of steering us toward the future He has planned, a future that is filled with hope, with purpose, and with blessings that we can't even begin to imagine.

Grace teaches us that failure is not the end; it is simply part of the journey. Every failure we experience is a lesson in disguise, a stepping stone toward the future that God has in store for us. Grace takes the broken pieces of our failures and uses them to build something new, something that reflects God's ability to redeem even the most hopeless situations. When we fail, grace steps in and whispers that our story is not over. It reminds us that God is still writing, still crafting, still shaping our future. Grace takes the places where we've fallen, the places where we feel like we've messed up beyond repair, and turns them into places of growth, of learning, and of new beginnings.

The waiting and the failures we experience in life are not wasted. God's grace is at work in every "not yet" and every "failure," turning them into something beautiful, something purposeful, something that points to His glory. Grace reminds us that God's timing is perfect, and that His plans for us are good, even when they don't align with our own. It teaches us to trust in the process, to trust in the waiting, and to trust that every "no" is simply a "not yet," and every failure is simply a step toward the future that God has prepared for us.

In the end, it is God's grace that defines our story, not the "no's" or the failures we face along the way. Grace is the pen that God uses to write the narrative of our lives, and it is a pen that never runs dry, never loses hope, and never gives up on us. God's grace is always at work, turning every "no" into "not yet" and every "failure" into "future," ensuring that our story is one of redemption, of hope, and of purpose. Even when we can't see it, even when we don't understand it, God is working, and His grace is crafting a future for us that is filled with His love, His goodness, and His perfect plan. And as long as grace holds the pen, we can trust that our story is far from over, and that the best is yet to come.

Chapter 17

"Each day is a new page, and grace is the author of every fresh start."

Each day is a new page, and grace is the author of every fresh start. As we rise each morning, the dawn of a new day greets us with the promise of endless possibilities, yet, so often, we carry the weight of yesterday's burdens—mistakes made, words spoken in haste, regrets that cling to our hearts, and failures that cast shadows over our hope for what could be. Life has a way of piling on disappointments, guilt, and frustration, leaving us feeling as though we are trapped in a never-ending cycle of the same struggles, the same disappointments, the same regrets. It's easy to believe that each day will be nothing more than a continuation of the last, that we will remain bound by the mistakes of our past or the worries that cloud our present. But God, in His infinite love and mercy, offers us something far greater than the weight of yesterday's failures—He offers us grace. And that grace is the author of each new day, writing on the blank pages of our lives with the ink of hope, mercy, and redemption. With God's grace, every morning is an opportunity for a fresh start, no matter how heavy the burdens of the day before may have been.

Grace is what transforms the ordinary into the extraordinary. It is what takes the broken, weary fragments of our lives and reshapes them into something beautiful and whole. No matter what happened yesterday, grace tells us that today is a new page, a chance to begin again, a chance to live with hope instead of fear, with love instead of regret. When we wake up, grace meets us like the gentle light of dawn, illuminating the path ahead, clearing away the remnants of yesterday's mistakes, and whispering the truth that God's mercies are new every morning. Lamentations 3:22-23 reminds us that it is because of the Lord's great love that we are not consumed, for His compassions never fail; they are new every morning. This is the promise that grace holds for us each day—that no matter how far we may have fallen, no matter how many times we have stumbled, God's grace is enough to pick us back up, dust us off, and set us on a new path filled with His love and purpose.

Every day we are given is a gift, a new chapter in the story of our lives that God is writing with His own hand. We may be tempted to believe that the mistakes we've made are too great, that we've already written ourselves into a corner, that there's no way to recover from the choices we regret. But grace tells us otherwise. Grace reminds us that God is not limited by our past, that He is always ready to write a new beginning for us, a fresh start that is filled with hope, healing, and restoration. No mistake is too big for God to redeem, no failure is too final for Him to rewrite. Each day is an invitation to turn the page, to step into the newness of God's grace, and to trust that He is still at work in our lives, crafting a story of redemption and purpose that far exceeds anything we could imagine for ourselves.

Grace is the great equalizer. It doesn't matter where we've come from, what we've done, or how many times we've fallen short—grace meets us right where we are and gives us the strength to start again. We may look at the pages of our past and see only a mess of failures, regrets, and missed opportunities, but grace sees something different. Grace sees potential, beauty, and a future filled with hope. When God's grace writes our story, He doesn't dwell on the mistakes of the past; He focuses on the promise of the future. He takes the broken, scribbled lines of our lives and rewrites them with words of healing, restoration, and purpose. Each day is a new page in this story, and with grace as the author, we can be confident that the ending will be one of redemption, hope, and love.

There is something incredibly freeing about the idea that each day is a new page, that we don't have to be defined by the mistakes we made yesterday. So often, we carry the weight of our past failures with us, believing that we are forever bound by the choices we've made. But grace breaks those chains. It tells us that we are not defined by our worst moments, but by God's love for us. It tells us that we don't have to live in the shadow of yesterday's regrets, but can step into the light of today's possibilities. With grace as the author of each new day, we are given the freedom to live without fear of failure, to take risks, to step out in faith, and to trust that God is with us every step of the way, guiding us, loving us, and helping us to grow into the people He created us to be.

Grace doesn't just offer us a second chance; it offers us countless chances. Each new day is a reminder that God's love for us is unending, that His grace is inexhaustible. We may stumble and fall, we may make the same mistakes over and over again, but God's grace never runs out. It is always there, always ready to pick us up, to forgive us, to set us back on the right path, and to give us the strength to keep going. Grace is not just a safety net for when we fall; it is the foundation on which we stand, the very thing that enables us to rise each morning with hope in our hearts, knowing that no matter what comes our way, God's grace is sufficient.

Every day is a new opportunity to experience the fullness of God's grace. It is a chance to let go of the guilt, shame, and fear that so often hold us back, and to step into the freedom that grace offers. We don't have to be perfect to receive God's grace; we don't have to have it all together. Grace meets us in our weakness, in our brokenness, and in our need, and it fills the gaps with God's love and mercy. It is grace that empowers us to live each day with courage, to face the challenges ahead with confidence, knowing that we are not alone. God is with us, and His grace is more than enough to carry us through whatever comes our way.

There will be days when we feel like we've failed, like we've fallen short of who we are supposed to be. There will be days when we feel overwhelmed by the weight of our responsibilities, by the pressures of life, by the expectations we place on ourselves. But grace tells us that we don't have to be perfect. We don't have to have all the answers or get everything right. God's grace is sufficient, and it is in our weakness that His strength is made perfect. Each day is a new page, and grace writes on that page with the truth that we are loved, that we are forgiven, that we are enough—not because of what we do, but because of who God is.

Grace gives us the freedom to live without fear of failure, to embrace each day as a gift, and to trust that God is at work in our lives, even when we can't see it. It reminds us that our story is not over, that each day is a new chapter in the book that God is writing, and that the ending will be one of hope, redemption, and love. Grace allows us to let go of the past, to release the mistakes we've made, and to step into the future with confidence, knowing that God is with us and that His plans for us are good.

As we wake up each morning and face the new day ahead, we can do so with the knowledge that grace is the author of every fresh start. Each day is a blank page, a new opportunity to live in the fullness of God's love and mercy.

We don't have to be held back by the mistakes of yesterday, because grace gives us the freedom to start again. Each day is a reminder that we are not defined by our failures, but by God's love for us. And as long as grace is writing the story, we can be confident that the pages of our lives will be filled with hope, healing, and the unending love of our Creator.

So, as we step into each new day, let us do so with gratitude for the gift of grace. Let us embrace the fresh start that God offers us, trusting that He is at work in our lives, crafting a story that is far more beautiful than anything we could write on our own. With grace as the author, each day is an opportunity to live with purpose, to love without fear, and to trust that God's mercies are new every morning. No matter what happened yesterday, today is a new day, a new page, and grace is already writing a story of hope, love, and redemption. And as we walk through the pages of our lives, we can rest in the assurance that grace is always enough, always present, always leading us toward the future that God has planned for us. Each day is a new page, and with grace as the author, the possibilities are endless, the hope is unshakable, and the love is eternal.

Chapter 18

"When we turn the page, grace greets us with the promise of something greater."

When we turn the page, grace greets us with the promise of something greater. Life often feels like a book filled with chapters that we may not have chosen, with twists and turns that catch us off guard, moments of joy interwoven with stretches of sorrow, and pages where the words seem heavy with disappointment or regret. We sometimes reach a point where it feels like the story we're living is stuck, where the same struggles, the same mistakes, and the same fears seem to repeat themselves, and we wonder if the next chapter will be any different from the last. We wonder if the failures of yesterday will follow us into tomorrow, or if the wounds we carry will ever heal. But grace is the faithful companion that walks with us through every page of our lives, whispering promises of hope, healing, and renewal. And when we find the courage to turn the page—when we decide to leave behind the weight of what was and step into the unknown of what could be—grace is there, waiting to greet us, assuring us that the next chapter holds the promise of something greater than we could ever imagine.

Grace is the reminder that no matter what has happened in the past, no matter how broken, lost, or uncertain we feel, there is always the possibility of a new beginning. It tells us that the story of our lives is not defined by the darkest moments or the most painful mistakes, but by God's unending love and His ability to redeem even the most difficult chapters. When we turn the page, grace assures us that the story is not over, that what lies ahead is not a continuation of our failures but the unfolding of God's perfect plan. Grace invites us to trust that the future is not limited by the past, that the pages we've already lived through are not the final word on who we are or what God has in store for us. Every new day, every new page, is an opportunity for God to write something new, something beautiful, something that reflects His grace and His goodness in our lives.

There are moments when turning the page feels impossible, when the weight of our current chapter seems too heavy to bear, and we wonder if we have the strength to move forward. Maybe it's the grief of loss, the sting of betrayal, the ache of dreams that haven't come true, or the fear of what lies ahead that holds us back. We might feel trapped in a season of pain or regret, afraid to let go of the familiar, even when it hurts, because the unknown feels too risky. But grace steps in and gently reminds us that we don't have to carry the weight of our past into the future. Grace tells us that God is doing a new thing, that He is working behind the scenes, even when we can't see it, and that turning the page doesn't mean abandoning what we've been through—it means trusting that God is going to use every part of our story, even the hardest parts, to create something greater. It means believing that what's coming next is not just more of the same, but something infused with God's promises of hope, restoration, and purpose.

Grace is the assurance that God's plan for our lives is greater than anything we could write for ourselves. When we turn the page, we are not stepping into an empty void; we are stepping into the pages that God has already written, pages filled with His love, His guidance, and His plans for our future. Jeremiah 29:11 reminds us that God knows the plans He has for us—plans to prosper us and not to harm us, plans to give us a future and a hope. When we turn the page, grace greets us with that promise, reminding us that the same God who has been with us in the past will continue to walk with us into the future, and that His plans for us are good, even when the path ahead is unclear.

The beauty of grace is that it meets us right where we are, in the middle of whatever chapter we're living through, and offers us the strength to turn the page, even when we're afraid. It doesn't force us forward; it invites us gently, offering us the assurance that we don't have to have all the answers or know what comes next. Grace tells us that it's okay to feel uncertain, it's okay to have doubts, and it's okay to be afraid. But it also reminds us that we are not alone. God is with us, and He is already at work in the next chapter, preparing a place for us that is filled with His peace, His provision, and His purpose. Grace gives us the courage to take the next step, to turn the page with the knowledge that whatever comes next, we are held in the loving hands of our Creator, and His grace will be sufficient for every moment ahead.

Sometimes, the hardest part of turning the page is letting go of the past. We hold onto our mistakes, our failures, and our regrets, believing that they define us. We replay the moments when we fell short, when we hurt others or were hurt ourselves, and we allow those moments to become the lens through which we view the future. But grace tells us a different story. Grace tells us that our past does not define us—God's love does. Grace tells us that we are not our mistakes, that we are not our failures, and that God's forgiveness is greater than any sin, any regret, or any shame we carry. When we turn the page, grace is there to remind us that we are new creations in Christ, that the old has passed away and the new has come (2 Corinthians 5:17). Grace wipes the slate clean and offers us a fresh start, a new beginning, a chance to live in the freedom of God's love rather than the chains of our past.

Turning the page is an act of faith. It's trusting that what lies ahead is in God's hands, that He is in control, and that His grace will be enough to carry us through whatever challenges we face. It's believing that even when we don't know what the future holds, we know the One who holds the future, and that is enough. Grace is the constant reminder that we don't have to walk this journey alone—that God is with us, guiding us, leading us, and providing for us every step of the way. When we turn the page, grace whispers that the best is yet to come, that God is not finished with us, and that the story He is writing for our lives is far greater than anything we could imagine.

There will be moments when the next chapter feels uncertain, when we don't know what to expect or how things will turn out. But grace invites us to trust in God's faithfulness, to believe that He is working all things together for good, even when we can't see it (Romans 8:28). Grace reminds us that God's timing is perfect, that His plans are better than our own, and that He is always working behind the scenes, weaving together the threads of our lives into a beautiful tapestry that reflects His love and His purpose. When we turn the page, grace greets us with the promise that God's plans for us are good, that He is with us in every season, and that He will never leave us or forsake us.

In the moments when we feel like we've reached the end of our rope, when we're tempted to believe that the story of our lives is stuck in a loop of disappointment or failure, grace offers us hope. Grace tells us that God is always writing, always creating, always working to bring about something greater in our lives. It reminds us that the story is not over, that the best chapters are still to come, and that God's grace is sufficient for whatever lies ahead. When we turn the page, grace is there, reminding us that each new day is an opportunity to experience God's love, to grow in faith, and to live out the purpose He has for our lives.

Grace is the promise that no matter how many times we've fallen, no matter how many times we've failed, there is always the possibility of something greater. It is the assurance that God is not finished with us, that He is still at work in our lives, and that the next chapter will be one of hope, healing, and restoration. Grace invites us to let go of the past, to release the fears and doubts that hold us back, and to step into the future with confidence, knowing that God is with us and that His grace is enough. When we turn the page, grace greets us with open arms, ready to write a story that is filled with God's love, His purpose, and His promise of something greater than we could ever imagine.

So, as we turn the page on the chapters of our lives, let us do so with faith, with hope, and with the knowledge that God's grace is always at work, writing a story that is far more beautiful, more redemptive, and more filled with love than anything we could write for ourselves. Let us trust that the next chapter will be one of growth, of healing, of restoration, and of new beginnings. And let us remember that no matter what lies ahead, God's grace will always be there to greet us, guiding us, sustaining us, and leading us into the promise of something greater.

Chapter 19

"Grace writes forgiveness where guilt used to stain the pages of our lives."

Grace writes forgiveness where guilt used to stain the pages of our lives. Every one of us carries moments, decisions, and actions that, when we reflect on them, fill us with guilt and shame. Guilt can feel like a heavy burden, a stain that seeps into the very fabric of our lives, coloring our view of ourselves and our future. It clings to our hearts, whispering that we are unworthy of love, unworthy of forgiveness, and unworthy of a fresh start. Guilt tells us that we are defined by our worst mistakes, that the pages of our story are irreversibly marked by the times we have failed, hurt others, or betrayed our own values. It can feel like a constant weight on our shoulders, dragging us down into despair, convincing us that our past mistakes disqualify us from the life we hoped for. But God's grace—so boundless, so transformative—enters into that mess and rewrites the narrative of our lives with the ink of forgiveness. Where guilt once stained every page, grace comes in and washes those stains clean, replacing the heavy burden of guilt with the lightness of forgiveness and freedom. In His hands, grace wipes away the marks of our failures and turns the story of our lives into one of redemption, hope, and second chances.

Grace does not ignore or gloss over the reality of our mistakes. It sees every moment where we have fallen short, every action that caused pain, and every wrong choice we have made. But instead of condemnation, grace offers us forgiveness. Instead of allowing guilt to have the final say, grace steps in and rewrites the ending. When we look at the pages of our past and see only the stains of guilt and shame, God sees the opportunity to show His love, mercy, and healing. Grace doesn't pretend that we didn't make mistakes, but it transforms the power those mistakes have over our lives. It takes what was once stained by guilt and turns it into a testimony of God's unending forgiveness and the freedom that comes from knowing we are no longer bound by the sins of our past.

Guilt is a powerful force, one that can shape the way we view ourselves and the world around us. It can distort our sense of worth, making us believe that we are nothing more than the sum of our worst moments. We replay those moments over and over again in our minds, trapped in a cycle of self-condemnation, believing that we are beyond redemption. But grace is even more powerful than guilt. Grace has the ability to break the chains of guilt, to lift the burden from our hearts, and to give us a fresh start. Where guilt once left us feeling unworthy and defeated, grace steps in and whispers, "You are forgiven. You are loved. You are free." Grace reminds us that we are not defined by our mistakes, but by God's love for us. And His love is greater than any guilt we carry.

One of the most beautiful aspects of grace is that it meets us right where we are, in the midst of our guilt and shame, and offers us forgiveness without condition. We don't have to earn God's forgiveness; we don't have to fix ourselves or clean up our mess before we can receive His grace. It is freely given, an outpouring of His love that covers every sin, every mistake, every regret. Grace takes the stained pages of our lives and writes over them with words of mercy and forgiveness, turning what once felt like a record of our failures into a story of redemption. Through grace, the guilt that once weighed us down is lifted, and we are given the freedom to move forward, unburdened by the past and filled with the hope of a future that is no longer marked by shame.

Forgiveness is at the very heart of grace. It is through forgiveness that grace does its most powerful work, healing the wounds we carry from our own mistakes and the mistakes of others. When guilt tells us that we are beyond redemption, that we have strayed too far from God's love, grace steps in and reminds us that nothing can separate us from the love of God. No sin, no failure, no mistake is too great for God's forgiveness. Grace writes forgiveness across the pages of our lives, covering the guilt and shame that once seemed so permanent. It reminds us that we are not prisoners to our past, but beloved children of God, forgiven and set free by His grace.

Guilt often leads us to believe that we must atone for our sins, that we must somehow make up for the wrongs we have done in order to be worthy of forgiveness. But grace tells us that the price has already been paid. Jesus, in

His great love for us, took the weight of our guilt upon Himself on the cross, offering us forgiveness that we could never earn on our own. It is through His sacrifice that we are made new, that the stains of our guilt are washed clean, and that we are given the gift of forgiveness. Grace is not about what we have done, but about what Christ has done for us. It is through His grace that we are able to turn the page on our past and step into a future filled with hope, healing, and the promise of new beginnings.

The stains of guilt may have once defined the story of our lives, but grace has the power to rewrite that story. When we surrender our guilt to God and allow His grace to work in our lives, we are no longer bound by the mistakes we have made. Instead, we are free to live in the fullness of His love and forgiveness. Grace doesn't just cover up the stains of guilt; it transforms them into something beautiful, something that reflects the redemptive power of God's love. Where guilt once weighed us down, grace lifts us up, giving us the strength to move forward with confidence, knowing that we are forgiven, that we are loved, and that we are free.

There is an incredible freedom that comes from knowing that our mistakes do not have the final word in our lives. Grace tells us that no matter how far we have fallen, no matter how many times we have failed, God's forgiveness is always available to us. We don't have to live in the shadow of our past mistakes; we can live in the light of God's grace. Each day is an opportunity to experience the freedom that comes from forgiveness, to let go of the guilt that has held us captive, and to embrace the new life that grace offers us. Grace writes a new story for our lives, one that is no longer defined by guilt and shame, but by the love and forgiveness of our Heavenly Father.

When we allow grace to write forgiveness over the pages of our lives, we are able to experience the fullness of God's love in a way that transforms us from the inside out. We no longer see ourselves as failures, but as redeemed children of God, forgiven and made new by His grace. The stains of guilt that once marred our hearts are washed away, replaced by the truth that we are loved, we are forgiven, and we are free. Grace doesn't just change the way we see ourselves; it changes the way we live. It frees us to love others as we have been loved, to forgive others as we have been forgiven, and to live each day in the light of God's grace, unburdened by the weight of guilt.

The story of our lives is not one of guilt and shame, but of grace and forgiveness. When we turn to God and receive His grace, we are given the gift of a new beginning, a fresh start where the stains of guilt no longer define us. Grace writes a new story for our lives, one that is filled with hope, healing, and the promise of God's unending love. We are no longer bound by the mistakes of our past; we are free to live in the fullness of God's forgiveness, knowing that we are loved, that we are forgiven, and that our story is one of redemption.

In the end, it is grace that has the final word. It is grace that takes the pages of our lives, once stained by guilt, and transforms them into a story of forgiveness, freedom, and love. And as long as grace holds the pen, we can trust that the story of our lives will always be one of redemption, one of hope, and one of unending love. God's grace is always at work, writing forgiveness where guilt once reigned, and giving us the freedom to live in the light of His love, forever free from the weight of guilt and shame.

Chapter 20

"God's grace writes through our fears, penning faith and courage in their place."

God's grace writes through our fears, penning faith and courage in their place. Fear is a force that touches every human heart at one point or another. It creeps in during moments of uncertainty, whispers lies in the stillness of the night, and wraps itself around our minds, convincing us that we are not enough, that we will fail, that life's challenges are too overwhelming, too great to overcome. We all face different kinds of fears—fear of the unknown, fear of failure, fear of rejection, fear of loss, fear that the future won't turn out as we hoped. These fears can become so deeply rooted in us that they begin to control the way we live, shaping our decisions, limiting our potential, and preventing us from stepping into the fullness of the life God has planned for us. But where fear seeks to paralyze and bind us, God's grace breaks through like a beacon of light, illuminating a different path. His grace doesn't merely brush aside our fears—it transforms them, rewriting the narrative of our hearts with words of faith and courage. Grace meets us in the very places where fear tries to take hold and instead fills those spaces with the boldness and trust that only come from God. Where we once trembled in the face of uncertainty, grace empowers us to walk forward with the assurance that we are never alone, that God's strength is made perfect in our weakness, and that faith can rise where fear once reigned.

Fear is a natural response to the challenges and uncertainties of life. It's a reaction that is deeply human, born out of our desire to protect ourselves from pain, from failure, from the unknown. But while fear may be a part of our human experience, it was never meant to be the defining force in our lives. God's grace steps in and begins to write a new story, one where fear does not have the final word. Grace teaches us that fear, while powerful, is not more powerful than the God who walks beside us. Grace shows us that we can face even the most daunting challenges, not because we are fearless, but because God's presence goes before us, His strength sustains us, and His promises hold us steady. It is through grace that we are able to see beyond the immediate circumstances that stir up fear in our hearts and instead focus on the truth that God is greater than any obstacle we face. Where fear seeks to close doors, grace opens them wide, inviting us to step out in faith, trusting that God is already at work, paving the way for us to walk in courage and boldness.

When fear rises up, it often speaks in absolutes. It tells us that we will never succeed, that we will never be good enough, that we will always fall short. Fear feeds on our insecurities, magnifying our weaknesses and making us believe that we are incapable of facing the challenges before us. But grace counters fear's lies with the truth of who we are in Christ. Grace tells us that we are more than conquerors through Him who loved us (Romans 8:37), that we are not defined by our fears but by the love and power of God working within us. It is grace that reminds us that we don't have to rely on our own strength to overcome fear. God, in His infinite mercy, gives us the strength, the wisdom, and the courage we need to face whatever comes our way. Grace writes through our fears, erasing the lies that seek to hold us back and replacing them with the truth of God's promises. It is through grace that we begin to see ourselves not as victims of our circumstances but as children of God, equipped with everything we need to stand firm in the face of fear and walk forward in faith.

There will always be moments in life when fear tries to creep back in, moments when the road ahead seems uncertain, and we feel overwhelmed by the weight of what lies before us. But even in those moments, God's grace is present, gently reminding us that fear does not have the power to define us. It is grace that lifts our heads, that strengthens our hearts, and that gives us the courage to keep going when we feel like giving up. Grace doesn't promise that we will never face fear, but it promises that fear will never have the final say. Where fear speaks of defeat, grace speaks of victory. Where fear whispers doubt, grace declares faith. And where fear paralyzes, grace moves us forward, step by step, into the future that God has prepared for us.

One of the most beautiful aspects of God's grace is that it meets us in our fears without condemnation. God knows our hearts; He knows the struggles we face and the fears that weigh heavily on us. But instead of scolding us for our fear, He offers us grace. He offers us His presence, His peace, and His power to overcome the very things that make us afraid. Grace doesn't demand that we be fearless; it invites us to bring our fears to God, to lay them at His feet, and to trust that He is bigger than whatever we are facing. Grace reminds us that we don't have to have it all together. We don't have to be strong on our own. God's grace is sufficient for us, and it is in our weakness that His strength is made perfect (2 Corinthians 12:9). When we allow grace to write through our fears, we find that our hearts are no longer ruled by anxiety or doubt, but by the steady assurance that God is in control and that He is working all things together for our good.

Courage is not the absence of fear; it is the decision to move forward in faith, even when fear is present. And it is grace that gives us the courage to take that step. Grace is what enables us to trust in God's goodness, even when we can't see the outcome. It is what allows us to walk in obedience, even when the path ahead is unclear. Grace teaches us that we don't have to wait until we feel fearless to act; we can step out in faith, trusting that God will meet us in our fear and give us the courage we need for the journey ahead. When grace writes through our fears, it replaces the paralysis of doubt with the boldness of faith. It reminds us that we are not alone in our struggles, that God is with us every step of the way, and that His grace is sufficient for whatever lies ahead.

Fear often tells us that we are inadequate, that we don't have what it takes to overcome the challenges before us. But grace speaks a different truth. Grace tells us that our adequacy is not found in ourselves but in Christ. It reminds us that we are equipped, not because of our own abilities, but because of God's power at work within us. Grace gives us the confidence to face the unknown, to step out into the deep waters of life, knowing that God is our anchor and that He will never let us drown. When we allow grace to write through our fears, we begin to see that the very things we were afraid of become opportunities for God to show His faithfulness, His provision, and His power in our lives.

There is freedom in knowing that we don't have to be bound by fear. We don't have to let fear dictate our decisions, limit our potential, or keep us from stepping into the fullness of what God has for us. Grace breaks the chains of fear and gives us the courage to live boldly, to dream big, and to trust God with every aspect of our lives. When fear tries to hold us back, grace moves us forward, reminding us that we are more than conquerors through Christ. It is grace that gives us the faith to believe that God is for us, that He is with us, and that nothing can separate us from His love. Grace writes through our fears, penning a story of faith, of courage, and of victory.

Even in the moments when fear feels overwhelming, when the challenges before us seem insurmountable, grace is there, gently guiding us forward, reminding us that we are not alone. God's grace is always present, always sufficient, and always working to replace our fears with faith. When we trust in His grace, we are able to face even the most daunting challenges with confidence, knowing that God is with us and that His plans for us are good. Grace doesn't promise that we will never face fear, but it does promise that fear will never have the final word. With grace as the author of our story, we can face the future with courage, knowing that God is writing a narrative of faith, hope, and love in our lives.

In the end, it is God's grace that defines us, not our fears. It is His grace that gives us the strength to move forward, the faith to trust in His plan, and the courage to face whatever comes our way. When we allow grace to write through our fears, we find that our hearts are no longer weighed down by doubt or anxiety, but are lifted up by the assurance that God is in control and that His grace is sufficient for every challenge we face. So, as we turn the page on the chapters of our lives, let us do so with the knowledge that grace is always at work, writing faith and courage into the very places where fear once held sway. And as long as grace holds the pen, we can trust that the story of our lives will be one of victory, of faith, and of the unshakable love of God.

Chapter 21

"Grace doesn't erase the past—it redeems it and writes a future full of hope."

Grace doesn't erase the past—it redeems it and writes a future full of hope. Life is a journey marked by both joy and sorrow, triumph and failure, peace and turmoil. Each of us has a past filled with memories—some that bring a smile to our faces, and others that weigh heavily on our hearts, memories we wish we could forget. There are moments in our lives we wish we could undo—choices made in haste, words spoken in anger, actions taken that led to pain, disappointment, and regret. It's in these moments, when we look back and see the mistakes we've made, the relationships we've broken, the paths we've taken that led us astray, that we often feel the burden of our past pressing down on us. We carry the guilt, the shame, the weight of those wrongs, and it can feel like our past defines who we are and limits the future we can hope for. But here's the beautiful, transformative truth of God's grace: grace doesn't simply wipe away the past as if it never happened—it redeems it. It takes all the broken pieces of our history, all the mistakes and failures, and turns them into something beautiful, something meaningful, something that points us toward a future filled with hope. In God's hands, our past is not a barrier to the future; it is the raw material from which He creates a new story of redemption and renewal.

The past is often a place we feel trapped in, replaying over and over the moments that we wish had gone differently, the opportunities missed, the relationships damaged. It's easy to feel stuck, believing that the person we once were, the things we once did, are unchangeable realities that will forever define us. But God's grace is bigger than our past, bigger than our mistakes, and more powerful than anything we have done or experienced. Grace doesn't erase the past because it doesn't need to. God doesn't need to pretend our mistakes never happened in order to love us, in order to redeem us, in order to give us a future that is filled with hope. Instead, grace takes all the mess, all the wrong turns, all the brokenness of our past, and redeems it. It transforms it. It uses it to shape us, to teach us, to grow us, and to bring us closer to God's purpose for our lives. What we often see as a series of failures, God sees as the foundation for something greater, something He is building in us that will reflect His love, His mercy, and His power to redeem.

There is something deeply comforting in knowing that God doesn't discard the broken parts of our past but instead uses them to write a future full of hope. Where we see mistakes, God sees opportunities for growth. Where we feel shame, God sees an invitation for healing. Where we feel regret, God sees a chance for redemption. Grace is not about erasing our history, as though pretending the painful moments never existed. Rather, grace takes those very moments, those experiences that we wish we could undo, and transforms them into something that serves God's greater purpose. The broken places in our lives become the very places where God's grace shines the brightest. It's in those areas where we have fallen short, where we have struggled, where we have experienced loss and heartache, that God's grace steps in and does its most powerful work. Grace doesn't sweep the past under the rug—it redeems it, reclaims it, and redefines it. The mistakes of yesterday don't have to be the mistakes of tomorrow because grace is at work, turning what was once broken into something beautiful and whole.

One of the most beautiful aspects of grace is that it doesn't ask us to forget the past—it invites us to see the past through the lens of God's love and mercy. Grace doesn't erase the pain we've felt or the wrongs we've done, but it changes the way those things affect us. Instead of allowing the guilt and shame of the past to weigh us down, grace lifts us up. It frees us from the burden of having to fix everything ourselves and reminds us that God is in the business of restoration. He is in the business of taking what was meant for harm and turning it into something good (Genesis 50:20). Grace is the reminder that our past, no matter how painful or difficult, does not have to define our future. With God, there is always the possibility of redemption, always the possibility of a new beginning, always the possibility of hope.

It's easy to believe that our mistakes disqualify us from the life we long for, that our failures have written us out of the future we hoped for. But grace tells us a different story. Grace tells us that no mistake is too big for God to redeem, no failure is too great for God to turn into something good. Grace doesn't simply erase the past as if it never happened; it transforms it into something that serves God's greater purpose in our lives. Every mistake, every wrong choice, every moment of brokenness becomes, in the hands of God, a tool for growth, for healing, for redemption. What we once thought would be our undoing becomes, through grace, the very thing that brings us closer to God, that deepens our faith, and that helps us to see the beauty of God's love and mercy more clearly.

When we look at our past through the eyes of grace, we see that nothing is wasted. The mistakes we've made, the pain we've endured, the lessons we've learned—all of it is used by God to shape us into the people He created us to be. Grace doesn't erase the past because it doesn't need to. God's love is so great, His power to redeem so profound, that He can take even the most painful, difficult parts of our history and turn them into something beautiful. Grace takes the guilt and shame of the past and replaces them with forgiveness and freedom. Grace takes the wounds of the past and heals them, leaving behind scars that are not marks of defeat but reminders of God's faithfulness and His power to heal and restore.

The future that grace writes is not one free from challenges or difficulties, but it is one filled with hope. Hope that comes from knowing that God is with us, that He is for us, and that He is working all things together for our good (Romans 8:28). Hope that comes from knowing that our past does not define us, that we are not bound by the mistakes we have made, but that we are defined by God's love and His grace. The future that grace writes is one where we can walk in freedom, knowing that we are forgiven, that we are loved, and that we are not alone. Grace gives us the courage to face the future with confidence, trusting that God is in control, that He has a plan for our lives, and that His plans are good.

Grace doesn't erase the past—it redeems it, and in doing so, it gives us the freedom to let go of the shame, guilt, and regret that once held us captive. We are no longer defined by the mistakes we have made or the wrongs we have done. We are defined by God's love, by His mercy, by His grace. The future that grace writes is one where we can live in the fullness of God's love, where we can walk in the freedom of forgiveness, and where we can experience the hope that comes from knowing that God is always with us, always working in our lives, always leading us toward a future that is filled with His love and His purpose.

In the end, grace is not about erasing the past—it's about transforming it. It's about taking the brokenness, the pain, the mistakes, and the failures and turning them into something beautiful. Grace is the power of God at work in our lives, redeeming what was once lost, healing what was once broken, and writing a future that is filled with hope, with purpose, and with the promise of God's unending love. No matter what has happened in the past, no matter how far we have fallen, grace assures us that the future is filled with hope because God is the one writing our story, and His plans for us are always good.

Chapter 22

"God's grace writes in the ink of love, sealing every chapter with His promises."

God's grace writes in the ink of love, sealing every chapter with His promises. From the very beginning of our lives, God has been writing a story for each of us, a story that is unique and filled with moments of joy, sorrow, triumph, and defeat. But through every page, every chapter, and every season of our lives, one thing remains constant: His grace. God's grace is the steady hand that writes on the pages of our hearts, crafting a story that is not defined by our failures, not limited by our weaknesses, but one that is written in the ink of His boundless love. That love is the very essence of grace—unearned, undeserved, and unending. And it is with this ink, the ink of His love, that God fills the pages of our lives with hope, healing, and redemption. Even when the narrative of our lives feels messy or incomplete, even when we stumble and fall, God's grace continues to write, sealing every chapter with His promises, reminding us that we are His, that we are loved, and that the story He is writing is far from over.

The beauty of grace is that it is not dependent on us—on how well we perform, on how perfect we try to be, or on how flawless our story appears. Grace is the gift of God's love poured out for us, freely given despite our shortcomings, and it is by grace that God writes the chapters of our lives. There are times when the pages of our story seem filled with pain, with loss, with mistakes that we wish we could erase. We may feel as though our lives are off course, as though the plot has veered far from the path we hoped for. Yet, even in those moments, grace is at work. God's grace doesn't erase the difficult chapters, but it redeems them. It takes the pages stained with regret and rewrites them with His love. It takes the broken places and seals them with His promises of restoration. It turns what we thought was the end of the story into the beginning of something new, something filled with hope and the assurance that God is with us, writing a future far greater than we could ever imagine.

Love is the ink that God uses because love is who He is. "God is love" (1 John 4:8), and His love for us is the foundation of everything He does. Every chapter of our lives is infused with His love, whether we realize it or not. Even in the darkest moments, when we feel lost, abandoned, or unworthy, God's love remains constant. His love doesn't waver when we make mistakes; it doesn't diminish when we doubt or when we fail. Instead, it is in those very moments that His love shines the brightest. God's love is the ink that rewrites the narrative of our lives, replacing fear with faith, sorrow with joy, and despair with hope. And because His love is eternal, the story He writes for us is sealed with promises that never fade, never weaken, and never end. God's promises are not fleeting words; they are eternal truths that anchor us, holding us steady even when life feels uncertain. He promises to be with us, to never leave us nor forsake us (Deuteronomy 31:6). He promises that His plans for us are good, plans to give us hope and a future (Jeremiah 29:11). These promises are the foundation of the story grace is writing, sealing each chapter with the assurance that we are deeply loved, eternally valued, and always held in His hands.

There are seasons in life when the chapters seem long and hard. When the story doesn't unfold the way we envisioned, we can be tempted to believe that God has forgotten us, that He has set the pen down and walked away. But grace tells us a different story. Grace reminds us that God is always at work, even when we cannot see it. He is writing a story that is far bigger than the immediate moment we are living in. Each chapter, even the difficult ones, has a purpose in His grand design. God's grace doesn't ignore the struggles we face; it embraces them, weaving them into a narrative that reveals His strength in our weakness, His peace in our chaos, and His love in our pain. Through grace, God takes the broken pieces of our lives and forms them into something beautiful. Each chapter of our story is sealed with the promise that God's love is greater than any trial we face, stronger than any fear we carry, and more powerful than any obstacle that stands in our way.

As God writes our story, His grace fills the pages with lessons that draw us closer to Him. Through moments of joy and moments of sorrow, grace teaches us to trust in God's timing, to rely on His wisdom, and to lean into His love. It's easy to trust God when life is going smoothly, but grace grows our faith in the seasons of uncertainty. When we don't understand the plot twists in our story, when we feel overwhelmed by the challenges we face, grace reminds us that God's hand is still at work, that the chapter we're in is not the end, and that His promises are sure. It is in the waiting, in the unanswered prayers, and in the moments when we feel stuck, that God's grace does its most transformative work. He writes faith on the pages of our doubt, hope in the midst of our despair, and peace in the midst of our storms. His love covers every word, every line, every chapter of our story, sealing it with the promise that He is not finished with us yet.

When we look back on the story of our lives, we may see chapters we wish we could rewrite, moments we wish we could undo. But grace tells us that those chapters are not wasted. God uses even our mistakes, even our failures, to bring about His purposes. He takes the parts of our story that we thought were too broken, too messy, too filled with regret, and He redeems them. Grace rewrites the narrative, turning what the enemy meant for harm into something good (Genesis 50:20). Each chapter of our lives, no matter how painful or difficult, is sealed with the promise that God is working all things together for good for those who love Him (Romans 8:28). His grace doesn't just brush over the hard parts; it transforms them, using them to shape us, to refine us, and to bring us closer to Him. God's love is the ink that turns our brokenness into beauty, our sorrow into joy, and our trials into testimonies of His faithfulness.

As God writes our story, His grace continually points us toward the future. He is not only the author of our past and present but of our future as well. Each chapter leads us closer to the fulfillment of His promises, to the future He has prepared for us. Grace gives us the confidence to look forward with hope, knowing that the God who began a good work in us will be faithful to complete it (Philippians 1:6). His love is the ink that writes the final word, and that word is victory. No matter what we face in this life, we know that the story ends with hope, with redemption, with eternal life in His presence. Every chapter of our lives, no matter how challenging, is sealed with the promise of God's unfailing love, a love that conquers all and that leads us to a future full of hope.

God's grace writes in the ink of love, and that love is the foundation of everything we are and everything we will be. It is the love that sent Jesus to the cross, the love that forgives our sins, the love that heals our hearts, and the love that secures our future. Every chapter of our lives is a testament to God's love and His faithfulness. When we feel unworthy, grace reminds us that God's love makes us worthy. When we feel lost, grace points us back to the promises of God, reminding us that He is our guide, our protector, our Savior. God's love is the ink that fills the pages of our lives with purpose, meaning, and hope. It is the ink that seals every chapter, assuring us that we are never alone, that we are always loved, and that our story is part of a much greater story—God's story of redemption for the world.

In the end, it is grace that defines our story. It is God's love that gives each chapter its meaning and purpose, and it is His promises that seal every page with hope. No matter what we have been through, no matter what lies ahead, we can trust that God's grace is writing a story that is filled with love, with redemption, and with the promise of a future that is secure in His hands. Every chapter of our lives, from the beginning to the end, is written in the ink of God's love, and His promises are the seal that guarantees that the story He is writing is one of hope, one of redemption, and one of eternal love.

Chapter 23

"Even when we can't see the ending, grace reminds us that the Author is good."

Even when we can't see the ending, grace reminds us that the Author is good. Life is a series of chapters, each one filled with its own blend of joy, sorrow, uncertainty, and hope. At times, the story of our lives feels clear and purposeful, like the path ahead is straight and smooth. But often, we find ourselves in the middle of chapters that are confusing, painful, or seemingly endless. We may face challenges that feel insurmountable—loss that we can't bear, disappointments that shatter our hopes, fears that loom so large we can't see around them. In those moments, it's easy to feel lost, to wonder where our story is heading, or to doubt whether there is any good that can come from the struggles we're enduring. We long to understand why things are happening the way they are, why God has allowed certain hardships, and how it will all work out in the end. Yet, in the midst of the uncertainty, when the future feels hidden and the ending seems far away, grace steps in as a quiet, steady voice reminding us that, even when we can't see the ending, the Author of our story is good. His goodness is not contingent on our circumstances or our ability to understand them. His goodness is woven into every line, every chapter, every twist and turn, even when we are too overwhelmed to see it.

Grace is what gives us the strength to keep moving forward when we don't know what's coming next. It's what anchors us when everything around us feels unstable, and it's what whispers to our hearts that God is still in control, still writing a story of redemption, even in the midst of our pain. Grace is the reminder that, no matter how dark or difficult the current chapter may be, the Author of our story is working all things together for good (Romans 8:28). His plans for us are not plans of harm or despair, but of hope and a future (Jeremiah 29:11). Even when we can't see the final pages, grace assures us that God is writing something beautiful, something that is far greater than we could imagine or understand. And while we may not be able to see the whole picture, we can trust that the One who holds the pen is faithful, loving, and good.

In the moments when we can't see the ending, when the present feels overwhelming and the future uncertain, grace is what carries us. It lifts our eyes beyond the present moment and invites us to trust in the goodness of God, even when we can't see how things will turn out. Grace reminds us that our story is not finished, and that the Author is still at work. We may only be able to see one page at a time, but God sees the entire book. He knows the beginning and the end, and He is guiding us through every chapter, using each experience to shape us, to teach us, and to draw us closer to Him. His grace is not just present in the moments of triumph and joy, but it is also at work in the valleys of our lives, in the hard seasons, in the moments of deep sorrow and confusion. Even when we feel lost or abandoned, grace tells us that God is still with us, that He has not forgotten us, and that His goodness is still writing the story of our lives.

There are times in life when we find ourselves in the middle of a chapter that feels unbearably hard. The road ahead seems long and uncertain, and we wonder how things will ever get better. We may face loss that breaks our hearts, struggles that test our faith, and challenges that leave us feeling helpless. In those moments, it's easy to wonder where God is, to feel as though we've been left alone to figure things out. But grace reminds us that God is not distant or detached from our pain. He is intimately involved in every detail of our lives, writing a story that is filled with His love and care. When we can't see the ending, grace tells us to trust the Author, to believe that He is good, and to know that He is working, even when we can't see how.

God's goodness is not always obvious in the midst of difficulty. There are times when we may question His plans, when we don't understand why He has allowed certain things to happen, or why the road has been so hard. But grace is what allows us to rest in the knowledge that, even when we don't have all the answers, God is still good. His goodness is not dependent on our ability to see the full picture. It is a fundamental part of who He is, and it is unchanging, even when our circumstances are not what we hoped for. Grace is what enables us to hold onto hope, even in the darkest chapters of our lives. It reminds us that the story is not over, that God is still writing, and that His goodness will be revealed in time.

One of the most powerful aspects of grace is that it meets us where we are, in the middle of the mess, in the midst of the uncertainty, and offers us peace. Grace doesn't require us to have everything figured out or to understand how the story will end. It simply invites us to trust the Author, to believe that God's heart is for us, and that His plans are always good, even when they don't make sense to us. Grace tells us that we don't have to see the ending in order to trust that it will be good, because we know the One who is writing it. God's goodness is the foundation of our faith, and grace is what allows us to rest in that goodness, even when life is hard.

When we are in the middle of a difficult chapter, it's easy to feel like things will never get better. We can become so focused on the present struggle that we lose sight of the bigger picture, of the story that God is writing. But grace gently lifts our gaze, reminding us that this chapter is not the whole story. There is more to come, and the Author is good. Grace tells us that the pain we're experiencing now is not the end of the story, that God is using even the hard things to shape us, to teach us, and to bring about something beautiful in our lives. We may not see the ending yet, but grace assures us that the One who is writing it is faithful, and that His plans for us are filled with hope.

As we walk through life, there will be seasons when we can't see the way forward, when the ending feels far away and unclear. But in those seasons, grace is what sustains us. It reminds us that we don't have to see the ending in order to trust the Author. God's goodness is not limited by our understanding, and His plans are not thwarted by our fears or doubts. Grace gives us the courage to keep going, to take the next step, even when we don't know what's around the corner. It is grace that reminds us that we are not alone, that God is with us, guiding us, and that His goodness will prevail in the end.

The beauty of grace is that it allows us to live with hope, even when we can't see the whole picture. It reminds us that God is writing a story that is far greater than we could ever imagine, and that His goodness is the thread that runs through every chapter. When we face uncertainty, when we are overwhelmed by the challenges before us, grace is what enables us to trust that the Author is good, that He knows what He's doing, and that the story He is writing is one of redemption, hope, and love.

Even when we can't see the ending, grace assures us that the Author is good, and that is enough. It's enough to carry us through the dark chapters, enough to sustain us when we are weary, and enough to give us hope when we feel lost. God's grace is always at work, always writing, always reminding us that His goodness is the foundation of our story. And because of His goodness, we can trust that the ending will be more beautiful than anything we could have imagined. No matter what we are going through, no matter how uncertain the future may feel, grace reminds us that the Author is good, and that is the promise we can hold onto. God's goodness will prevail, His love will triumph, and His grace will carry us through to the end of the story, where we will see, with clear eyes, that every chapter was filled with His goodness, His love, and His faithfulness.

Chapter 24

"Through every trial and triumph, the pen of grace writes a story of everlasting love."

Through every trial and triumph, the pen of grace writes a story of everlasting love. Life, in all its complexity, is like a book filled with pages of joy and sorrow, victory and defeat, love and loss. Each of us is living a story, one that is full of twists and turns, unexpected challenges, and moments of breathtaking beauty. Sometimes, the chapters we go through feel like they were written with ease—moments where everything seems to fall into place, where blessings flow, and where joy seems effortless. But other times, the pages are filled with trials so heavy that they weigh on our hearts like a burden too great to bear. It is in these moments of difficulty, when we are in the valley of hardship and pain, that the pen of grace steps in, unseen yet always present, to weave a narrative that reflects not just our experiences but the deeper truth of God's enduring love. Grace, in all its power and beauty, is the thread that ties every part of our story together, reminding us that no matter what we face—whether it be moments of triumph or seasons of trial—God's love is the constant, unchanging force that carries us through. It is through His grace that our lives are transformed into stories of redemption, hope, and everlasting love, no matter how many broken chapters there may be.

Grace is the gift we receive in both the highs and lows of life. It is easy to see grace in the triumphs—when prayers are answered, when healing comes, when success follows hard work, and when we can clearly see the hand of God blessing us. In those moments, we feel God's love radiating through every good thing we experience. But the beauty of grace is that it is not limited to the times when life is easy or when things go our way. Grace is just as present in the trials, in the moments of pain, confusion, and loss. It is through grace that we are carried when we can no longer carry ourselves, when the weight of the world feels too heavy, and when hope seems distant. In those times, the pen of grace continues to write, not erasing the pain or the difficulty, but redeeming it, transforming it into something meaningful, something that points us back to the everlasting love of God. Grace writes a story in which no trial is wasted, no tear is in vain, and no hardship is too great for God's love to overcome.

When we face trials, it's natural to wonder why. Why did this happen? Why am I going through this? Where is God in the middle of my suffering? In those moments, we may feel abandoned, alone, or confused, as though the narrative of our lives has taken a turn that we didn't expect and don't understand. But even in those moments, grace is at work. Grace doesn't always provide the answers we seek in the moment, but it always provides the assurance that God is with us, that His love is unshakable, and that He is writing a story that is far bigger and more beautiful than we can see. Every trial we endure is a chapter in that story, and through grace, those chapters are not just filled with pain, but with purpose. Grace doesn't erase the difficulties we face, but it transforms them, giving them meaning in the broader context of God's everlasting love. Through grace, we are reminded that even in our darkest moments, God's love is still present, still powerful, and still at work in our lives.

The triumphs we experience in life—those moments of victory, of joy, of success—are also written with the pen of grace. It is by grace that we are able to celebrate the good things in life, to enjoy the blessings that come our way, and to experience the joy that fills our hearts when things are going well. But grace also keeps us grounded, reminding us that these triumphs are not just the result of our own efforts or abilities, but of God's love and favor. It is through grace that we recognize that every good gift comes from above (James 1:17), that the triumphs we experience are not just random strokes of luck or chance, but are part of the story God is writing in our lives. Grace reminds us to be grateful, to recognize the hand of God in our victories, and to remember that His love is the source of all good things.

Grace is the pen that writes a story in which every moment—whether it be one of joy or sorrow—is woven into the greater narrative of God's love. Through every trial and triumph, grace is at work, shaping us, molding us, and drawing us closer to the heart of God. The trials we face teach us to rely on God, to trust in His goodness even when we can't see the full picture, and to find hope in His promises. The triumphs we experience remind us of His faithfulness, His provision, and His desire to bless His children. In both the good and the bad, grace is what sustains us, what carries us through, and what reminds us that we are part of a story that is so much bigger than we can imagine—a story that is ultimately about God's everlasting love for us.

Sometimes, we are tempted to believe that our story is defined by the trials we face. We may look at the challenges in our lives and feel like they overshadow everything else, that the pain, the struggles, the hardships are what define who we are. But grace tells us a different story. Grace tells us that our lives are not defined by our trials, but by God's love. It is His love that holds us together when everything else seems to be falling apart. It is His love that gives us the strength to keep going when we feel like giving up. It is His love that reminds us that we are never alone, that He is with us in every season, in every chapter, writing a story of redemption, of hope, and of love. Grace takes the trials we face and transforms them into opportunities for God's love to shine even brighter in our lives. It is through the trials that we come to understand the depth of God's love, the power of His grace, and the strength of His promises.

The triumphs we experience are also part of the story of grace. They are the moments when we see God's hand at work in clear and tangible ways, when we are reminded of His goodness and faithfulness. But grace doesn't just leave us in the triumphs—it points us back to the source of those victories, reminding us that it is God's love that has carried us, that has blessed us, and that continues to write our story. Grace teaches us to hold our triumphs lightly, recognizing that they are gifts from God, and to be humble in our successes, knowing that it is by His grace that we have achieved anything at all. It is through grace that we are able to celebrate our triumphs without becoming prideful, and to give thanks to God for the blessings He has poured out in our lives.

Through every trial and triumph, grace writes a story that is ultimately about God's everlasting love. It is a love that never fails, that never gives up, and that never lets go. It is a love that is present in every chapter of our lives, whether we are walking through the valley of the shadow of death or standing on the mountaintop of victory. God's love is the constant, unchanging force that carries us through every season, and it is by grace that we come to know and experience that love in deeper and more profound ways. Grace is what takes the trials and triumphs of our lives and weaves them into a story that reflects the beauty, the power, and the depth of God's love for us.

Even when we don't understand the trials we are facing, even when the road ahead seems uncertain, grace reminds us that God is still writing our story, that He is still at work, and that His love is the foundation of everything He does. Every trial is an opportunity for us to experience God's love in new and deeper ways, to see His faithfulness, and to trust in His promises. Every triumph is a reminder of His goodness, His provision, and His desire to bless us. And through it all, grace is the pen that writes the story of our lives, a story that is ultimately about the everlasting love of God.

In the end, it is not the trials or the triumphs that define us—it is God's love. It is His grace that carries us through every season, that writes the story of our lives, and that seals every chapter with the promise of His love. Through every trial and triumph, the pen of grace writes a story of everlasting love, a story that is filled with hope, with redemption, and with the assurance that we are loved by a God who never gives up on us. And as long as grace holds the pen, we can trust that the story of our lives will be one that reflects the beauty, the power, and the unending love of God.

Conclusion

As we reach the conclusion of "From Brokenness to Beauty: Written by the Pen of Grace", it is important to remember that the journey of faith is not a destination, but an ongoing walk with God. The transformation from brokenness to beauty is a process, and while you may have experienced healing, redemption, or renewal in certain areas of your life, there will always be new challenges, new trials, and new opportunities for God's grace to work in you. This book has taken you through the reality that, no matter how deep your pain or how fragmented your story, God's grace has been there all along, writing beauty into every broken part. But the story is not over. God's grace is not done yet.

As you continue your walk with God, remember that grace is not a one-time event; it is the lifeblood of your faith. Every step you take, whether through valleys of despair or mountaintops of joy, will be held together by the same grace that has brought you this far. You may still encounter moments of brokenness—times when you feel weak, lost, or unsure of what comes next. But in those moments, lean into God's promises, knowing that His grace is sufficient for you, and His strength is made perfect in your weakness (2 Corinthians 12:9). When you feel overwhelmed, remember that the pen of grace is still writing, still turning your trials into testimonies, and still transforming your pain into purpose.

Walking with God requires courage—courage to trust Him even when you can't see the way forward, courage to surrender your brokenness into His hands, and courage to believe that His plan for your life is greater than anything you could imagine. It means daily choosing to allow the beauty of God's grace to define you, not your past, not your mistakes, and not your fears. It means walking by faith, knowing that the God who began a good work in you will carry it on to completion (Philippians 1:6).

So, as you continue on this journey, may you walk in the assurance that God is with you, that He is still writing your story, and that His grace will carry you through every season. Let your life be a testament to His love, His faithfulness, and His power to take even the most broken parts of us and transform them into something beautiful. Keep walking, keep trusting, and keep allowing God's grace to write the story of your life—one chapter of beauty, redemption, and faith after another.

Don't miss out!

Visit the website below and you can sign up to receive emails whenever Joshua Rhoades publishes a new book. There's no charge and no obligation.

https://books2read.com/r/B-A-AJLBB-CKGBF

BOOKS 2 READ

Connecting independent readers to independent writers.

Did you love *From Brokenness To Beauty Written By The Pen of Grace*? Then you should read *Anchored In Truth Exploring The Depths of Psalm 119*[1] by Joshua Rhoades!

"Anchored in Truth: Exploring the Depths of Psalm 119" is an invitation to dive into one of the Bible's most profound passages, offering a deep exploration of faith, devotion, and the transformative power of God's Word. As the longest chapter in the Bible, Psalm 119 is a masterpiece of spiritual expression, structured as an intricate acrostic with each section beginning with a letter of the Hebrew alphabet. This psalm is not just a collection of verses; it is a meditation on the beauty and necessity of God's law. Through its 176 verses, the psalmist reveals a fervent love for God's commandments, a deep dependence on His guidance, and an unyielding pursuit of understanding and wisdom found only in the Scriptures.

"Anchored in Truth" invites you to explore the rich themes of Psalm 119, offering insights into how God's Word can shape, guide, and sustain a life of faith. This book is crafted not just to help you understand the words of this ancient psalm but to experience them in a way that profoundly impacts your daily walk with God. As you journey through each section, you will see how the psalmist's experiences resonate with the challenges and triumphs of your own spiritual life—whether it's seeking deliverance in trials, finding delight in God's statutes, or pleading for divine guidance.

---

1. https://books2read.com/u/mvPayX

2. https://books2read.com/u/mvPayX

This book is more than an intellectual study; it is a call to transformation. Psalm 119 urges us to anchor our lives in the unchanging truth of God's Word, making it the foundation of our character, decisions, and ultimate hope. The psalmist's devotion to God's law reminds us that Scripture is not just a set of rules or a historical text; it is the living Word of God, active and relevant in every aspect of our lives.

"Anchored in Truth" aims to inspire you to cultivate a deeper love for God's Word, seek His guidance in all things, and live out the truths found in these verses. As you read, may you be encouraged to stand firm in the faith, anchored in the unshakable truths of God's Word, and experience the wisdom, peace, and joy that come from living in alignment with His eternal commands.